D0000836

/—

Quest for Quality

How One Company Put Theory to Work

ROGER L. HALE
President and Chief Executive Officer

DOUGLAS R. HOELSCHER
Vice President
Engineering/Manufacturing/Purchasing

RONALD E. KOWAL
Director
Manufacturing/Purchasing

Tennant Company
Minneapolis, Minnesota

Second Printing

Susan Mundale, Editor
Pine and Mundale Inc.
Minneapolis, Minnesota

Kevin Pederson, Designer
Pederson Design
Minneapolis, Minnesota

Rita Maehling, Project Director
Tennant Company

This book is dedicated to the many generations of Tennant Company employees, at all levels of the company, who have truly believed in people as the foundation of a good enterprise. This belief has formed the culture in which a quality emphasis could take root and grow.

Contents

Foreword

Tom Peters

The lead article in the February 18, 1987 *New York Times* business section started this way: "For the first time since 1924 the Ford Motor Company is back as the most profitable automobile company in America." The reasons for Ford's relative surge, of course, are complex. But chief among them, in my mind, is the payoff from Ford's quality improvement program. Though all of the Big Three have improved, Ford's gains have been dramatic, vaulting it to the top of the heap in the United States by a long shot.

The good news from Ford is an island amid despair. The eclipse of American business, from steel to semiconductors to banking, is frightening. Some economists estimate that as many as 30 million people have been dislocated because of our decline in the last 15 years. Real wages for 25- to 34-year-old males dropped 26 percent between 1973 and 1983.

Unfair trade practices of other countries may have hurt us some, but the plain fact is that from Silicon Valley to Detroit, we've come up short on quality. Poor quality and the management inattention that has induced it rank far ahead of Tokyo, Washington, or union headquarters as a cause of our precipitous decline.

So what do we do? The good news is that some companies are coming back. The best news is that some who have accepted the challenge to become world-class competitors are willing to share the secrets of their journey with us. For that reason, I am delighted to introduce you, the reader of *Quest for Quality*, to the story of Tennant Company's eight-year adventure in not just quality improvement, but in making quality, as they say, "the only thing—or at least first among equals, the equals being cost and schedule."

The Tennant Company story is one of passionate commitment, persistence, wholesale people involvement—and sound management systems and problem-solving techniques. The results so far of this "marathon, not ... sprint" are compelling. Manufacturing rework dropped from 33,000 hours to 6,800 hours between 1980 and 1986. Supplier reject rates, resulting from partnership programs mounted with suppliers, plummeted from 6.8 percent in 1980 to 1.7 percent in 1986. Progress has been great enough to allow introduction of an unprecedented warranty program.

The details of technique are in this book. The reader learns about Tennant Company's reward systems, involvement programs, and guidelines for setting up teams. Vignettes about specific, extraordinary small-group efforts dot the book and are unfailingly instructive.

The second section of the book is the most important, as far as I'm concerned. It starts this way: "The how-to's of quality are not difficult to master." What's tough, the seasoned Tennant Company team declares, is instilling "the five most important factors for success." They are: management commitment; employee involvement; cooperative, nonadversarial worker/manager relationships; rewards for people; and time, energy, and determination.

All texts and case studies on quality improvement pay lip service to these five in some form or other, but most then rush ahead to the pros and cons of voluntary versus nonvoluntary teams, the details of Ishikawa diagram construction, and so on. *Quest for Quality* makes it clear, and in vivid detail, that the five key factors deserve the most attention; they add up to a revolution in attitude and minute-by-minute ways of doing business.

For example, top management had a difficult time at first convincing managers that this was not just another "motivational program." They attacked the problem in part by altering executive incentive programs so that they included incentives for the achievement of hard-nosed, quantitative quality improvement goals. Then there was the difficulty, that almost all such programs have faced, of getting marketing, sales, and field service people as engaged as factory workers in the program.

True employee involvement faced monumental hurdles as well. The authors admit, "In the past we hired people to do their jobs and nothing else. In fact, we frowned on any activity *except* the job." Now, suddenly, the worker was being asked to contribute ideas; moreover, ideas that went beyond his or her 25 square feet of work space.

First-line supervisors had an even tougher time adapting to the change from cop to listener and facilitator, from protector to destroyer of old and sacrosanct functional barriers. Indeed, as the book makes painfully clear, the most profound shift was from an adversarial to a cooperative mind set—between workers and managers, among functional groups on the organizational chart, and between suppliers and Tennant Company.

The most compelling message that emerges is the need to keep pounding away. Tennant Company presents case study after case study that end with astonishing results—results that took, in solving even narrow gauge problems, five or six years to accomplish, with numerous teams formed and dissolved, suppliers slowly pruned from a bunch to one or two, and so on.

If world-class quality is to be achieved, all business leaders in America, in manufacturing or service, need to ask themselves if they are ready to make the thoroughgoing commitment to a whole new way of life that the Tennant Company saga suggests is necessary. Tennant Company executives liken it to dieting—and then the even harder challenge of keeping the weight off!

Do we have a choice? I think not, if we care about the economic legacy we wish to leave behind to our children and grandchildren.

Chief Executive Roger Hale grabbed my attention quickly when he recounted a story about a problem in 1979 with one of his most successful products. "Why were the hydraulic leaks happening only in the machines we sent to Japan and not in those we were selling in the U.S., where, in fact, we were selling many *more* of the same machines? As it turned out, the leaks weren't just happening in Japan. The machines we sold here at home were leaking too. The difference was that U.S. customers accepted the leaks. If a drop of oil appeared on a freshly polished floor, they simply wiped it up. In Japan, the leak was cause for complaint. Japanese customers expected better quality.... At about the same time, we faced our first serious competition from Japan from the lift-truck division of Toyota when it announced its entry into the sweeper business."

If that doesn't give each of us cause for reflection, I don't know what would. Sadly, many have faced the same music that Hale heard—and either have done nothing or have launched a major program with great fanfare that has fizzled in six months, consigned to the notorious "program of the year" graveyard that haunts most executive suites.

Commitment, patience, persistence, a wide array of tools—and a healthy dose of terror—that's what it's taking at Tennant Company. Yet these superstars feel that they've barely begun.

Are you ready to sign up for the marathon?

Preface
Roger L. Hale

In 1979, Tennant Company embarked on a quest—a search for higher productivity in manufacturing, support and sales, higher quality in our products, and better working relationships between managers and employees.

We didn't begin our quest out of desperate need. Our company, nearly 110 years old, had respectable sales of $100 million in a relatively small industry. Our products—powered floor sweepers, scrubbers and scarifiers, and floor coatings—were already regarded as the best of their kind. We were small enough to enjoy goodwill between management and employees throughout the company, both in our corporate headquarters in Minneapolis where our administrative, engineering, and domestic manufacturing facilities are located, and in our plants, sales offices, and distribution centers in the United States, South America, Europe, and Japan.

Like many companies in the late 1970s, we had been working on productivity in an effort to be more cost effective. We had a steering committee of six executives looking at various ways to improve productivity. We tried traditional methods, such as pumping life into our 40-year-old employee suggestion program, and a number of specific cost-reduction and productivity improvement projects. All of these efforts were successful, and many of them remain in use today. Still, we weren't satisfied.

Then, in the spring of 1979, I attended a trade association meeting in Washington, D.C. On the program was a speaker who made an informal presentation to a group of 50 executives. The speaker's name was Phil Crosby, and his subject was quality. Crosby had just left ITT, where he had been a corporate vice president for worldwide quality. He was setting himself up in business as a consultant, and that presentation must have been one of his first efforts at marketing his services. I was intrigued.

When I returned to Minneapolis, I called our vice president for manufacturing to tell him about Crosby. To my surprise, I learned that Doug Hoelscher had read Crosby's book (*Quality is Free*) and had already invited him to visit the company.

That was good news for a couple of reasons. Like all CEOs, I tend to gain energy from seminars and meetings with other executives. Sometimes the people we work with actually dread our going off to those events because we come back full of enthusiasm and new ideas. The memos fly for a week or two, and once in a while we even inspire a little enthusiasm. Most of the time, though, people go through the motions and hope that life will return to normal before long.

A similar process happens in reverse. In just about any company, there are hundreds of good ideas generated every year that never go anywhere because the executives aren't interested. I know that has happened at Tennant Company, and I'm sure it has happened where you work. So when a good idea surfaces in more than one place, it has a much better chance of succeeding than when it comes from only one source.

Another reason I was happy to hear about Crosby's visit to our company had to do with some complaints about the quality of one of our company's products. As I said earlier, Tennant Company was known for producing top-quality floor maintenance equipment. But during my visits with our Japanese joint-venture partner in the late 1970s, I had been hearing complaints—sometimes bitter complaints—about hydraulic leaks in our most successful machines. Back home, I began asking questions: Why were the hydraulic leaks happening only in the machines we sent to Japan and not in those we were selling in the U.S., where, in fact, we were selling many *more* of the same machine?

As it turned out, the leaks weren't just happening in Japan. The machines we sold here at home were leaking too. The difference was that U.S. customers accepted the leaks. If a drop of oil appeared on a freshly polished floor, they simply wiped it up. In Japan, the leak was cause for complaint. Japanese customers expected better quality. That really set me thinking.

At about the same time, we faced our first serious competition in Japan from the lift-truck division of Toyota when it announced its entry into the sweeper business. The news spread in our company, and suddenly everything we'd been hearing about Japanese cars, Japanese stereos, and Japanese television sets versus U.S. cars, stereos, and television sets began to take on new meaning. Before long, quality was more than just another program at Tennant Company. We saw that a potential competitor's product could affect our jobs and our livelihood.

Those events, all happening in 1979, motivated us to begin our journey toward quality. We have found that like all important ideas, quality is very simple. So simple, in fact, that it is difficult for people to understand.

Let me explain. Suppose a friend tells you he is going to describe the workings of a computer to you. You know this isn't going to be easy, so you get yourself ready for a struggle. On the other hand, if that friend tells you he is going to explain a pencil to you, you say to yourself, "I already know what a pencil is." No matter what your friend tells you, it will be hard to dislodge your preconceived notions about the pencil.

The notion of quality is like that of the pencil. Most people know what quality means. The problem is that everyone's notion is different. It's not easy to get people thinking about quality in a new way, especially when quality is such a "simple" idea to grasp.

Now I'm going to appear to contradict myself by saying that quality is also very complicated. Changing the quality of a product or the quality of people's work life is a step into the unknown. It requires commitment from everyone involved, and commitment isn't easy when the idea you're asking people to commit to is so difficult to explain. It requires developing methods of measuring quality—or lack of it—sometimes in minute increments. It requires developing measurements in some aspects of work, particularly in non-manufacturing areas and the upper levels of management, that have never been measured before. It requires commitment to training and development, and to staying with it even when you're forced to cut back in other areas. It requires the solid backing of every member of the management team. It requires setting goals and measuring progress toward them. It requires the long view, and the ability to appreciate incremental gains that may not seem significant at the time. Quality is a marathon, not a sprint.

Even though we have had some struggles and difficulties, Tennant Company's journey in quality has been a rewarding adventure. Along the way, we have made unexpected and exciting discoveries. Most have to do with the tremendous power and potential, in the people who do the work, for solving existing problems. More than anything, an organized emphasis on quality helps a company tap that power.

Over the years, we have received many requests from other companies to share our experience in quality. We do that in a number of ways. We sponsor an annual meeting and conference with the Japan Management Association. We invite representatives from other companies to visit our facilities. We believe that by exchanging information, we can learn from one another. This book is another way of sharing what we have learned. We hope you will find in it something of value. But please don't keep your quality efforts a secret. Let us know what you do. No doubt there will be much in your experience that we, at Tennant Company, can use in our continuing quest for quality.

Roger L. Hale, President and Chief Executive Officer
Tennant Company
March 1987

Our thanks to Philip Crosby and *Quality Is Free*, McGraw-Hill Book Company, 1979.

Introduction

Philip B. Crosby

On the day I was preparing to leave ITT in 1979, I received a call from Doug Hoelscher asking if I would be able to help Tennant Company install a quality improvement effort. Representatives from IBM had talked to me the same day, and I had arranged to go see them the following week. My decision to set up a consulting firm seemed to be working out although, as of that moment, I had no office, no staff, no products, and very little money. But I felt that my experience within ITT in dealing with dozens of businesses had prepared me for both computers and sweepers.

We arranged for me to come to Minneapolis where I met Roger Hale, Tennant Company's CEO, and the rest of his team members. I was impressed with the genuineness (and that is a carefully chosen word) of all of them. They were open and sincere in their concern about quality. They were also used to working with consultants, and I saw an opportunity to learn a lot from them about business.

The facilities were immaculate, and the people were intensely going about their business. As we toured the plant and huddled in offices, it became clear to me that they were working very hard on the conventional systems of quality. The seven assembly lines emptied into a large inspection and test station. From there, all the sweepers that had been assembled and tested went to the rework station.

The rework station really could be in capital letters. Like most American plants, it was a permanent fixture containing the most experienced workers available, and it was busy all the time. I knew right away it had to go.

It was at this point that I began to see why Tennant Company was a different kind of company with a very different attitude. These people really listened to what I had to say, got a clear understanding of my reasons, and then they actually did what I suggested. This was a new experience for me. For my whole career, I had been watching people improve only half as much as they could because they only took half the advice they should.

We went to work on the present problems by identifying all the defects and plowing them back to the source to get them eliminated. This included eliminating the rework station with the idea of having the assembly line make the product right the first time.

By that time I had completed arrangements to hold the first Quality College classes at Rollins College in Winter Park, Florida. The classes were 18 people each and I planned for one a month. (Now we have a dozen each week worldwide.) Tennant Company sent people to class until all of their key folks attended and began to commonly understand that quality was a practical and attainable fact, not some mysterious, unmeasurable commodity.

In my mind, the success Tennant Company has had over these past years is attributable to three things.

First, there was an authentic management interest in dramatically improving quality. For them it was a matter of survival, and they recognized that the conventional ways of ensuring quality just did not change things.

Second, they were willing to learn and then act.

Third, they selected good quality teams and were patient while the implementation process moved along. They did not decrease their efforts as improvement began to emerge, and they continually encouraged these team members.

My relationship with Tennant Company has always been special for me. In those days I was on my own. Now we have several hundred people, many locations, products for all applications, and a great deal of experience. I don't get to do much "hands-on" these days.

Also, in the beginning of Philip Crosby Associates, when we were having the cash flow problems that go with starting up, Tennant Company was supportive enough to pay us in advance. You don't find many like that; I have always remembered their consideration.

I know you will find this to be an interesting book.

ONE

THE TENNANT COMPANY STORY

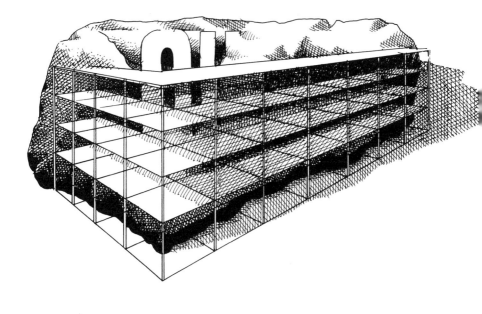

THE TENNANT
COMPANY STORY

Quality means identifying the requirements of the job, finding a way to measure whether or not they're being met, and meeting the requirements by doing things right the first time.

Quality has become a major concern of American business. At Tennant Company, we began focusing on quality in the late 1970s. Like many other manufacturers, we were doing some hard thinking about our ability to stay competitive in what was rapidly becoming a world marketplace. The 1974-75 recession had taught all of us, as individuals and businesses, that we were vulnerable to forces over which we had little control—like the Arab oil embargo and a zooming inflation rate that could decimate even the most well-planned budget.

At the same time, many industries were beginning to feel the bite of foreign competition, particularly from Japan. Japanese automobiles were being purchased by Americans looking for smaller, more efficient and dependable cars. Japanese television receivers and stereos were undercutting sales of American-made electronics products. Japanese industry was being hailed as the most forward looking and productive in the world. Japan's post-World War II image as the maker of cheap goods had been completely turned around. Now, Japanese products were known for their quality and reliability—and their superiority over American products.

For most manufacturing companies, the late 1970s and early 1980s were a time of self-examination. If there were so many uncontrollable outside forces that could affect us, we reasoned, we'd better begin looking inward at our own methods and processes to see what could be improved. At Tennant Company, productivity seemed a logical place to start. Unlike the price of oil or low labor costs in developing countries, productivity was something we *could* change. In 1978, we organized a steering committee of six executives to see what could be done.

The steering committee began by paring the costs of some operations and reviving our employee suggestion program. But we quickly learned that productivity wasn't going to improve with a few programs or budget adjustments. The more we looked at productivity, the more we were troubled by questions we couldn't answer: How do you measure improved productivity? Or low productivity, for that matter? If you do make some gains, how can you sustain them? How do you involve the people who do the work, instead of imposing changes upon them?

We made some progress over the next few months, but our efforts seemed fragmented. We knew there had to be a better approach somewhere, a "pearl" of wisdom that would point us in the right direction.

Our "pearl" turned out to be a book by Philip B. Crosby, *Quality is Free*. The book contains a "quality management maturity grid" that helps a company identify where it is in terms of quality—from "Stage I: Uncertainty" through "Stage V: Certainty," with "Awakening," "Enlightenment," and "Wisdom" in between. The grid measures several aspects of the quality improvement process: management's understanding and attitude; the importance of quality to the organization; the way problems are handled; the cost of quality as a percent of sales; what is done to improve quality; and the words generally used to summarize the company's stance regarding quality.

By applying Crosby's grid to our company, we discovered we were indeed spending and wasting time, energy, and resources to make quality products. Our assembly area was a good example. Our process there went something like this: Assembly, inspection. Rework, inspection.

Rework again, inspection again. It became obvious that in assembling our products, we certainly weren't doing things right the first time. It wasn't that the assembly people were inept or careless about their work—far from it. In fact, assembly employees were some of the most skilled and experienced in the company. They were doing the best job they could, given the procedures and equipment the company provided. The problem was that we had allowed extensive rework to become an integral part of our manufacturing process. By 1978, we were employing 18 rework people in assembly—at an average annual wage of $16,000. We were reworking quality into our products, and at considerable cost.

Phil Crosby says that quality is free. It took us a long time to figure out what he meant, because it was clear to us that the quality of our products was costing money. Like other manufacturers, Tennant Company was absorbing the cost of scrapped parts, warranties, engineering changes, and computer re-programming, all the result of not doing things right the first time. Crosby says that these are not quality but "unquality" things, and the cost of "unquality"—when time, energy, and resources must be applied to correct things not done right the first time—usually runs between 20 and 25 percent of total sales for most companies. Some quick calculations showed that for a company the size of ours, this could amount to more than $25 million a year. "*Quality* is not only free," Crosby says, "it is an honest-to-goodness profit maker. Every penny you don't spend on doing things wrong, over, or instead becomes half a penny right on the bottom line."

One of the tools Crosby has created to help his clients focus on quality is the concept of zero defects. The theme of zero defects is "do it right the first time." That means preventing defects rather than just fixing them. According to Crosby, zero defects can be achieved in all areas of a company, from manufacturing to service, from office support to sales. By working toward accomplishing every job with zero defects, a company reduces the cost of *not* doing things right the first time.

By 1979, we were moving out of the stage Crosby calls "uncertainty" into "awakening." We were ready for the first big step in our journey toward quality. We invited Crosby, who had left ITT to become an independent consultant, to teach us the concept of zero defects as a tool for quality improvement. Crosby was not our only teacher. We adopted—and still use—statistical quality concepts learned in seminars with other productivity and quality experts, including W. Edwards Deming and Joseph M. Juran. We were drawn to Crosby's overall approach, however, because it could be applied in all segments of our company, from manufacturing to office and field operations. Crosby offered a unified approach to three areas on which we wanted to work: problem solving, cost reduction, and quality improvement. Most important, we chose Crosby's approach because it emphasizes quality *management* more than quality *control*. We were convinced that management was the key to improved productivity and quality.

The Tennant Company management team made a commitment to having Crosby help us get started and set direction by spending one day a month with us for the first year. He walked the team through the ideas in his book. We wrestled with the definition of quality for our company. We finally agreed that quality means identifying the requirements of the job, finding a way to measure whether or not they're being met, and meeting the requirements by doing things right the first time. When we had consensus on what quality meant to us, we drew up a policy statement that was printed and signed by our president, Roger Hale. It reads:

> *It is the policy of Tennant Company that quality management shall exist in each operational area. By quality management we mean that each operational area shall perform its functions exactly as required or shall cause the requirements to be officially changed to what we and our customers really need.*

Making that pledge public was the second step in our journey. Executives are not always visible to all employees on a day-to-day basis; therefore, we as managers decided to publicize our commitment so employees at all levels knew about the pledge. We posted the signed pledge, and people across the company began to read and hear and, we hoped, to think about quality.

Testing the Water

Before the year was over, we decided to try some of Crosby's zero-defects principles and techniques. We initiated three pilot programs, one in production and two with suppliers.

In production, we assembled a small group of mechanics and some engineers with specialties in design, quality, and manufacturing to streamline production of our Model 432 walk-behind automatic scrubber. We believed it was important to have our first pilot project in manufacturing so we could bring hourly people and supervisors into the quality effort as soon as possible. The automatic scrubber was chosen *not* because it was particularly defect ridden, but because it was a higher volume product with many repetitive manufacturing steps that could be quantified and studied. In addition, the supervisor in the manufacturing area where the 432 was produced was known as a risk-taker willing to try new ideas.

The group began by studying ways to assemble the scrubber more efficiently, with the objective of building as much of the machine as possible—including sub-assembly parts—on the line. (Previously, orders were filled from the sub-assembly area and the parts were moved to the stockroom, then back to assembly when needed.) By the time they finished, group members had completely rearranged the assembly line so the Model 432 could be built and crated all in the same area. That meant an annual saving for Tennant Company of more than $19,000 in storage space, reduced lead time, and lowered inventory carrying costs. The improved efficiency also reduced the rate of defects in the finished product. When the project began, the Model 432 averaged 1.3 defects per machine; at the end of the first year, the number of defects per machine was reduced to 0.42.

In the pilot projects with suppliers, we focused on two short-term goals: 1) increasing the number of zero-defect engines received from a group of our largest suppliers; and 2) raising the percentage of governors received with zero defects from one particular supplier who agreed to work closely with us. Within a year, we had increased the number of zero-defect industrial engines received from our suppliers from 49 percent to 66 percent, and the number of defect-free governors received had risen from 75 to 90 percent. We were gaining confidence in our zero-defects procedures, and we decided it was time to broaden the scope of our efforts.

The First Quality Team

Early in 1980, we brought together representatives from all departments of the company to form our first Quality Team. Members of that first team were hand picked, because we knew the success of our efforts hinged on their ability to work together and get the job done. (Since then, we have asked for volunteers for each successive company-wide team—and every time we ask, we have more volunteers than can serve on the team.)

All of the team members were middle managers. They were people we knew would be willing to take on extra responsibilities in addition to their regular jobs. The manager of manufacturing engineering, who was also our productivity manager, was asked to lead the team. The team's charge was to implement Phil Crosby's 14-step program (see appendix), as outlined in *Quality is Free*, in all areas of operation: engineering, systems, personnel, manufacturing, international, marketing, finance, quality control, purchasing, administration, and sales.

The team outlined its goals: 1) to establish a quality management program in every operation, 2) to eliminate surprise nonconformances, and 3) to reduce the cost of quality to no more than 2.5 percent of sales by 1988. The first step in accomplishing those goals was to train the company's officers, managers, and supervisors to use the principles and techniques of Crosby's 14 steps in their work areas.

Identifying the Barriers

First we had to identify barriers to quality improvement—that is, problems that prevented people from doing their jobs right the first time. We combined two of Crosby's steps: Step 6: Corrective Action (To provide a systematic method of resolving forever the problems that are identified through previous action steps) and Step 11: Error-Cause Removal (To give the individual employee a method of communicating to management the situations that make it difficult for the employee to meet the pledge to improve). We created the Tennant Company Error Cause Identification (ECI) Form (see appendix) on which employees described the problem that prevented them from doing their jobs right the first time. They sent the form to an ECI coordinator, who routed it to the proper person in engineering, manufacturing, or administration for action.

First, we had to identify problems that prevented people from doing their jobs right the first time.

The response was overwhelming. In the first six months of 1980, the coordinators had received 1,200 ECI forms—each identifying a problem that prevented someone in the company from doing his or her job as well as possible. The list was a litany of defects: The print is wrong. The weld symbol is wrong. The adhesive doesn't hold. The heating coil clamps aren't working. Form after form, each filled out by an employee hoping the problem would be corrected.

Most of the problems identified on ECI forms required attention from engineers. For a time, the people in engineering tried to follow up on each ECI form in person. They even staged a "Super Saturday," when every member of the department came in to try to get to the bottom of the stack and initiate some improvement for each problem. Finally, engineering had to declare a six-week moratorium on new ECIs just so the department could catch up.

It became clear that solving the problems identified on the ECI forms was only a "band-aid" approach. We needed to work on our procedures and methods so those problems would be *prevented*, not just fixed. We began to see that the only way to do that was to involve the people who were doing the work. And to solve problems successfully, we needed specific instruction in working together in groups.

We turned to the Japanese because of their use of quality circles as a teamwork approach. We learned that the most useful information about quality circles had been compiled by the Japanese Union of Scientists and Engineers (JUSE), and that it had been translated into English by W.S. Reiker and published by Quality Control Circles, Inc., of Saratoga, California. We began using those translations—the basic course (we call it the "red book") and the advanced course (the "blue book")—to train people in the operations areas in small group problem-solving skills. The specific tools we adapted from the JUSE materials are described in the third section of this book.

Adapting those materials was not our only contact with Japanese manufacturers. In 1980, we invited a group of Japan Management Association members touring the United States to visit our company. Most were middle managers facing the same problems we were. During their visit, the group's leader, a distinguished industrialist named Mr. Kinoshita, made a brief speech to a group of managers and supervisors. The quality effort had been successful in Japan, he said, because it provided a way for people to have some control over their jobs. Kinoshita, retired chairman of the Hitachi Ship Building Company, emphasized that the purpose of the zero-defects program is not only to create defect-free products, but to enhance the work life of employees. His speech helped us understand some of the deeper aspects of the quality effort.

Measuring the Cost of Quality

Before we could begin working on problems related to quality, we needed a reference point to tell us whether or not we were improving. We also had to measure the cost of quality for Tennant Company. In every department, we began tracking procedures that we believed contributed to the cost of not doing things right the first time. We also looked at overall manufacturing indicators, such as defects per machine prior to shipment, warranty expense, the number of hours spent in rework, and the rate of rejected purchased part lots. We looked at the percentage of orders shipped the same day they were received, at inventory accuracy in the field warehouse, and at the number of machines delivered defect free to the customer. We also looked at the number of hydraulic joint leaks per machine. With these indicators identified, we could begin to measure our progress.

Brazilian Bungle

One of my most valuable lessons about quality came through an incident that had all the makings of an international crisis. It started early one morning with a telephone call—the kind you know from instinct is important, so you answer before anyone else can.

The voice at the other end was growling. "Kowal, we have problems!" The call was from a manager in our international department. A container load of parts and supplies shipped to our manufacturing plant in Brazil was being held by the Brazilian government. There was a discrepancy between what we said was in the container and what was actually inside. Parts had been misidentified and miscounted. The government was sure we were smuggling parts into the country. The manager at our manufacturing plant in Brazil was facing expensive fines because of the errors, and he had expressed the desire to put his hands around my neck for just 15 seconds.

My first reaction was to call the manager of material handling and pounce on him. Of course he would then call the supervisor and do the same to him. Finally the supervisor would find out who caused the error and pounce on the people who packed and shipped the container.

Would the problem be solved? Would pinning the blame on the employees who actually packed the container accomplish anything? The answer to both questions was no. The cause—or the blame—did not belong to the employees. It was ours as managers. We have come to believe that people do not intentionally make mistakes. When mistakes are made, it is usually due to lack of proper tools, training, or time.

As managers, it is our duty to provide employees with the proper tools and training to get the job done. We can achieve zero defects by conveying our attitude that quality is important. We do that in the attention we pay to jobs and people.

The container shipment story had a happy ending. Approximately four weeks after the Brazilian incident, four employees from the stockroom came to see me with some ideas about how the job *should* be done. The result of their efforts is described later in this book. More importantly, this incident provided tangible proof that a quality effort pays off. **R.K.**

The Power of Small Groups

Armed with practical problem-solving tools, small groups of employees formed throughout the company to work on problems in specific areas. The first group was made up of four stockroom employees. They addressed one of Tennant Company's biggest non-manufacturing problem areas: the shipping of parts for TENNANT® machines to overseas customers and our manufacturing plants in such far-flung places as Australia, Japan, and Brazil. The group was formed after a shipment of parts to Brazil had been held by the Brazilian government because our documents did not correctly identify all the material in the container.

Using its newly learned problem-solving skills, the group pinpointed the problems and developed alternative solutions. The members saw that the task of packing parts in containers for overseas shipment was badly organized, and they saw a lack of communication among the various work groups involved. They also realized they were operating without adequate equipment and space. To make matters worse, there were no well-defined procedures outlining responsibilities and time schedules.

To solve their problems, they changed the way the work was done. Gathering of parts for one shipment became one person's job, and accuracy increased. The work space for packing was expanded, and needed equipment was purchased. The group also put together a training program for new stockroom people.

The results were dramatic. Accuracy of shipments rose to 100 percent. The number of orders shipped within 48 hours rose to 72 percent of orders received. Given the constraints of the system (when the orders come out of the computer, when the mail truck comes in, etc.), 75 percent is the maximum that can be expected.

Another pilot group tackled our most persistent and embarrassing problem: oil leaks from the hydraulic joints in the machines we produced. During Phil Crosby's first visit to Tennant Company, we (Doug and Phil) spent two hours touring the assembly area. As we walked through, Crosby

TENNANT® is a registered trademark of Tennant Company. The ® should appear with this name on all typed or printed material, whether for use inside or outside the company.

asked employees, "What's your biggest problem?" The most frequent answer was, "Hydraulic oil leaks." In fact, when we asked one engineer what to do about the leaks, he could only recommend a large drip pan under every machine. It was an appropriate problem with which to begin our manufacturing quality emphasis.

We formed a small group of five people: a product design engineer, a quality assurance engineer, a person from assembly, a trainer from personnel, and the vice president of manufacturing as a management representative.

Instead of jumping in with solutions as we would have in the past, we put our new problem-solving skills (described in detail later in this book) to use. Group members met weekly for six months to study improvements in training, engineering, and purchasing. Their first job was to define, for Tennant Company, just what "hydraulic oil leak" meant. The answer:

An oil leak is *one drop* of oil falling from a hydraulic joint during *one hour* of machine operation at normal operating temperature and pressure.

By most standards, the leaks we were so concerned about would not be considered a problem. But for our purposes, even one drop of oil is too many. In 1979, we averaged one oil leak for every 75 joints assembled. The average machine has 150 joints, so we were averaging two leaky joints per machine. Most were caught before the machine was shipped to the customer, but each one required rework and, as a result, cost us money in employees' time and delayed delivery. The consequences of hydraulic leaks spread far beyond the assembly area.

Having defined the problem, the next step was to make a cause-and-effect diagram. The diagram told us we had deficiencies in several areas:
- **Methods** of tightening hydraulic joints during assembly. Most methods were passed verbally from one employee to another.
- **Materials.** Our purchasing people had been buying hydraulic fittings and hoses from no less than 16 different suppliers. Each

part number had been purchased from the supplier who offered the lowest per piece cost. No wonder the parts didn't always fit together properly.

- **Training.** The people responsible for assembling hydraulic joints had never been trained in the correct method. They used the principle that if tight was good, tighter must be better. And with the quality emphasis, everyone was trying to do better.
- **Design.** In the past, design engineers had put extremely low priority on hydraulic joints. The design group viewed hoses as something that connected the really important parts of the product such as pumps, valves, and motors. The routing of hoses, the ease with which they could be connected, the number of joints, and the fitting and hose specifications were of virtually no concern to the design engineers.

After determining the causes of hydraulic leaks, the group set some short- and long-term goals. Overall, they decided on a three-pronged approach: 1) training for every worker who handled parts for the machines' hydraulic system; 2) reducing the number of suppliers of hoses and fittings from 16 to 2 to assure greater uniformity and, we hoped, focus the suppliers' attention on the quality of their products; and 3) re-engineering the hydraulic system to include fewer joints, and, therefore, fewer places that could leak. The team worked with the two suppliers to come up with a method of marking joints so an inspector could quickly see whether or not they had been properly tightened.

The group members outlined what they would do to solve the problem, then set goals:

- **Trainer.** Short-term: Develop training programs for engineers and assemblers. Long-term: Train all engineers, assemblers, supervisors, and managers. Do a refresher update every other year.
- **Designer.** Short-term: Develop specifications for all hoses and fittings used on current products. Set goals to reduce and simplify fittings on current products. Long-term: Set goals for specific number of joint fittings on all new products and for involving assembly people in initial product design.
- **Assembler.** Short-term: Actively participate in the development

of the training program. Long-term: Assist in all training sessions as a co-trainer. Be available every day to answer questions and assist in solving day-to-day problems.

- **Quality Assurance Engineer.** Short-term: Collect data and keep score. Actively participate in the development of the training program. Long-term: Collect data and keep score. Assist in all training sessions as a co-trainer. Be chief communicator of both positive and negative issues and trends.
- **Management.** Short-term: Remove roadblocks and provide necessary resources. Long-term: Remove roadblocks and provide necessary resources.
- **Team.** Long-term: Eliminate hydraulic leaks in five years.

The following chart shows the team's progress year by year. In brief, by 1981, we managed to reduce the number of leaks to one for every 216 joints. Improvements were less dramatic from then on, but better design and procedures made it possible to reduce leaks to one per 1,286 joints by 1985. That year, for the first time, there was not

HYDRAULIC CONNECTION LEAKS

1 LEAK IN 2800 JOINTS

1 LEAK IN 611 JOINTS

1 LEAK IN 619 JOINTS

1 LEAK IN 1286 JOINTS

1 LEAK IN 509 JOINTS

1 LEAK IN 216 JOINTS

1 LEAK IN 100 JOINTS

one leak reported from any joint in any machine in the field. We had turned an embarrassing problem into an achievement that received industry recognition. In 1984, the National Fluid Power Association honored us with its PRO award. The original small group responsible for reducing hydraulic leaks continues to make sure our gains are maintained. Around Tennant Company, they're known as the guardian angels of hydraulic leaks.

1981: Team learned about hydraulics, including the best assembly methods

Team set own goals

Average performance: 1 leak per 216 joints

1982: Developed extensive training programs

Developed and printed training manuals

Trained managers, supervisors, assemblers, and engineers

Purchasing department set supplier goals

Replumbed test machines with new methods; reduced number of joints and overall fitting and hose costs by 10 percent per machine

Average performance: 1 leak per 509 joints

1983: Reduced number of hydraulic hose and fitting suppliers from 16 to 2

Average performance: 1 leak per 611 joints

Worked with suppliers to replumb current product line and new products

1984: Introduced newly plumbed products at year-end

Average performance: 1 leak per 619 joints

Received National Fluid Power Association's PRO Award for our work in this area

1985: Gave training update to all assembly people

Reduced number of suppliers from 2 to 1, which also reduced hose and fitting costs by 10 percent

Average performance: 1 leak in 1,286 joints

Not one customer reported a leak from any machine shipped this year

1986: Average performance: 1 leak per 2,800 joints

Zero field-reported leaks

Like Fine Furniture

We confronted another major problem for Tennant Company during our first year with the quality emphasis. That problem was the number of machines damaged in shipment.

Our sales people pride themselves on being present when machines are delivered to their customers. Needless to say, they weren't happy when a machine showed damage from shipping or proved defective when rolled onto the customer's floor or outdoor surface for the first time. The situation was particularly sticky if the customer happened to be in our international market, far from our manufacturing facility in Minneapolis with its replacement parts and new machines.

We gathered a group of people from industrial engineering, shipping and receiving, design engineering, international sales, marketing, purchasing, and quality control to address this problem. Dubbed the Crating Task Force, the group began by examining every procedure involved in crating a TENNANT machine and shipping it to the customer. The next steps were to identify how and why damages occurred and to recommend corrective action. As a result of the group's work, the percentage of machines damaged in shipment dropped from more than 5 percent in 1980 to less than 1 percent in 1983.

Members of the shipping department didn't stop there, however. They believed they could find a way to ship machines *uncrated* and get them to their destinations without defects. Their solution was to treat every TENNANT machine like a piece of fine furniture, transporting it directly from the company's loading dock to the customer's dock wrapped in padded quilts and packed in a moving van equipped with air-cushioned suspension. By 1985, 17 percent of our machines were being shipped crateless at a savings of $89,000 per year.

Celebrating Success: ZD Day I

The successes of our first year with the quality emphasis gave us the confidence that we were on the right path, even though we were just beginning. So we began planning our first Zero Defects (ZD) Day celebration for February 1981. The purpose behind the celebration was not to motivate or entertain people. Our intent was only to let employees know that something important was happening, and that they would all have the chance to get involved.

That first ZD Day event was held at Orchestra Hall, in downtown Minneapolis. We hired 30 buses to transport every Minneapolis employee to the event, and we shut down the company for half a day to make sure everyone could go. A bluegrass band played in the lobby as people entered. During the program, Minnesota Congressman Bill Frenzel and Bob Lurtsema, a popular sports and television personality, gave talks, as did one of our plant managers and one of our customers. Finally Roger Hale, Tennant Company's president, said a few words. He told everyone about the pilot projects and the progress we'd made. He explained management's commitment to quality, and announced that everyone in the company would be asked to make the same commitment. Then we all got on the buses and returned to work.

Back at work, everyone was asked to make a personal pledge to do the job right the first time. More than 99 percent of the work force signed the pledge, which included commitment to the following goals.

We will:
1. Make quality first among equals (with costs and schedules).
2. Make "doing the job right the first time" routine procedure.
3. Make TENNANT the standard for quality worldwide.
4. Make Zero Defects our performance standard.
5. Make our quality system defect prevention, not fire fighting.
6. Make it everyone's responsibility to eliminate a problem that inhibits our quality objectives.

Suppliers—A Key Element

Early in the quality emphasis, we realized we could not improve the quality of Tennant Company products without paying attention to the component parts made by other companies. (More than 65 percent of our product cost is made up of materials and parts purchased from 1,100 suppliers.) We were convinced that the impact of suppliers on the quality of our products was too large to ignore.

In 1981 we began a supplier quality emphasis program. First, we decided to choose suppliers on the basis of product quality as well as competitive cost. We outlined three goals to guide us in our supplier relationships:

1. Suppliers have the responsibility to deliver exactly the product and/or service they've promised to provide.
2. Suppliers are expected to provide defect-free products.
3. If problems arise, suppliers must satisfy all complaints fully and quickly, then correct the system that caused the problem.

But when we began studying our relationships with suppliers, we found that *we* were largely responsible for the problems they had in supplying us with defect-free parts. Unclear specifications, incorrect testing, and misapplication of components all contributed to failures and rejects. We knew we had to work together to bring about change.

We started our supplier program by inviting the top-level executives from 20 key vendor companies to visit Tennant Company during

PURCHASED PART REJECT RATE

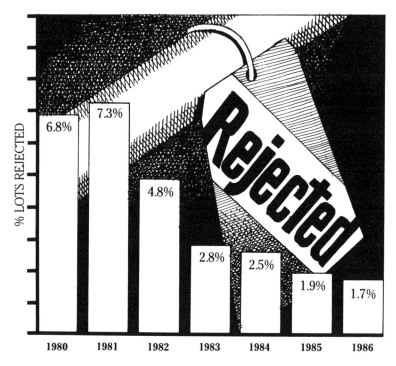

% LOTS REJECTED

6.8% — 1980
7.3% — 1981
4.8% — 1982
2.8% — 1983
2.5% — 1984
1.9% — 1985
1.7% — 1986

Supplier I: Going to the Top

Two years or so into our quality emphasis, we began to realize that long-term, sustained success could only be achieved with the co-operation of suppliers. Why? Because a substantial portion of our products are made of parts purchased from other companies. In fact, 65 percent of the cost of our manufactured products is from purchased materials. We were continually complaining about the quality of the products we received.

When I began to look further into our relationships with suppliers, a number of issues emerged:

- Our engineers seemed to be continually working on the same design problems, but never really solving them.
- Those problems surfaced at random, then went away for a while, then reappeared.
- Our top managers and those of our key suppliers were not involved in supplier relationships. They only became aware of problems if production schedules were not being met.
- All of our key suppliers were much larger than Tennant Company.
- Our purchases were a very small percentage of their total revenues.
- We had no idea how to do any better with suppliers in the future than we had done in the past.
- We had an idea that the problems we were blaming on suppliers may not have been entirely caused by them.

Through our work with the quality emphasis, I often turned to Phil Crosby when I wanted to talk things over or think out loud about a problem. I asked Phil where he thought I might begin.

He responded by telling me a story. When his children were young, Crosby's wife bought most of their clothes, plus other household items, from a large national department store. When there were problems with the merchandise or service she never called the salesperson or the department manager, or even the store manager. She called the president of the organization, a multi-billion-dollar corporation. "If she can call the president of a company," Crosby asked, "why can't you?"

Why not? I got the phone number of our largest supplier—not surprisingly, the one with whom we were having the largest number of quality-related problems. I was apprehensive about calling the president to tell him that there "might be" some quality-related problems with his product that he "might not" know about.

His response: "Why the hell are you calling me? I have people to handle these kinds of things."

I took a deep breath and explained that at Tennant Company we were trying a new approach. Our CEO and I wanted to become more involved with our counterparts in key supplier companies, and we had set a goal of reducing our supplier base by 10 percent per year over the next five years. I seemed to have his attention. I told him I hoped he was interested in keeping our business and invited him to a meeting. He reluctantly agreed.

At the meeting, we showed him documentation outlining the percentage of parts received from his company that we had to reject because of poor workmanship. It became obvious to him that the product he was selling was not of the quality his people had led him to believe. His shoulders drooped. "What do you want me to do?" he asked.

"Ship us the product as promised," we said. We then explained that we didn't expect zero-defects products immediately, and that we could work with him to meet our expectations. We had three requirements:

1. Set annual improvement goals.
2. Meet with us annually to review progress against those goals.
3. Become a fully qualified supplier by meeting those goals.

In turn, we said, we would send him semi-annual reports showing his company's performance. As long as he continued to show improvement and eventually became qualified, we would continue to purchase from him.

The result has been a much more satisfying relationship with a key supplier. His company did set and meet goals. We continue to purchase parts from them, and they are a part of our group of major suppliers. We now provide quarterly updates to each of that group, and many participate in our ZD Day programs. Meeting our quality goals has become a joint effort. When a company depends as we do on outsiders for so many components of its products, cooperation for quality not only makes sense, it is absolutely essential. **D.H.**

the course of the year, so we could explain our quality emphasis and review their quality records. These companies were invited because of the dollar volume of our purchases from them, the impact of their potential nonconformance on finished product quality, and the volume of their nonconformance to Tennant Company standards. In other words, we invited those suppliers who had the biggest nonconformance problems. Their response to the invitation was enthusiastic.

We held three pilot meetings for suppliers in 1981—called Zero Defect Awareness Days. We focused on sharing information and ideas. At the end of each meeting, we asked the suppliers to commit to a quality improvement goal that would improve their companies' performance.

Every one of the 20 suppliers committed to quality goals, and most succeeded in improving their performance. One engine supplier improved its quality level by 57 percent. Another company, which manufactures hydraulic cylinders, cut its level of defects from 6.4 percent to 0.8 percent, and a supplier of small hydraulic motors decreased defects from 8.8 percent to 2.3 percent. Since 1981, we have developed a detailed process for evaluating and working with suppliers. It includes on-site assessment of the supplier's management structure and overall business operations, a discussion about the quality process with top management, mutual agreement about Tennant Company's requirements, and specific criteria for reliability, incoming lots, piece parts, and delivery. (See appendix for a summary of the Supplier Qualification Process.)

The Tennant Company purchasing department places each supplier in one of the following categories:

1. **Qualified.** The highest rating a supplier can obtain. To achieve this rating, the supplier must meet all of the evaluation criteria.

2. **Conditionally Qualified.** The supplier does not meet one or more of the criteria. Suppliers in this category are informed of the conditions that must be met before they will be moved into qualified status, as well as the time frame in which the conditions must be met. New and existing product parts will not be assigned to conditionally qualified suppliers unless qualified suppliers cannot provide them.

Suppliers II: The Top 20

After the positive response we received from our largest supplier, we decided to go through the same process with the other 19 of our top 20. During the next year, I met personally with either the CEO or, if our supplier was a division of a large, multi-division corporation, the president or general manager of that division.

I asked each of them to set annual improvement goals and to meet with us annually to review them. I received enthusiastic responses from all but one supplier—and that company no longer makes parts for Tennant Company. (It became apparent that the person at the top didn't really understand what we were doing or why we needed his involvement. Because he wasn't completely committed to quality, the response we received from his people and the quality of the parts they made fell below our standards.)

Over the next four years, we saw substantial improvement in the quality of the parts we purchased from those top 20 suppliers. We decided to go one step further.

During those four years, the cost of our materials had increased at approximately the same rate as inflation. (We use the Producer's Price Index for Intermediate Materials as a measure.) We decided to set some cost-containment goals so future cost increases would be at a fraction of inflation.

Again, we went to each of our key suppliers. We asked them to make cost-containment commitments to help us meet our goals. It was during one of those visits that I had one of the most heart-warming experiences of my 25 years in this business.

My contact was one of the co-founders of a company that had been acquired and was now a division of a very large corporation. He had stayed with the company as the division's general manager, and when I visited him, he was celebrating 40 years in manufacturing.

He welcomed me with a warm handshake and a simple statement: "Doug, I owe you. You started us on our own quality emphasis four years ago by telling us the quality of our products might not be what we thought it was or would want it to be. You made us look at what we were doing and how we were doing it, and as a result we started a quality emphasis of our own. Thanks to you, we will be able to reduce our prices by 3.3 percent this year and an additional 6.4 percent next year."

I couldn't have heard a more satisfying testimonial to the effectiveness of a quality process. That supplier continues to make high-quality parts for us. In fact, when we began the quality process, we divided our business for the part he supplied between his company and two others. Since then, we have discontinued our relationships with the other two, and we now buy that particular part only from his company. **D.H.**

3. **Unqualified.** If the supplier does not meet any of the criteria, and if continuous improvement is not shown, the supplier is placed in unqualified status. If improvement is not seen, steps are taken to discontinue the business relationship.

We place a great deal of importance on our relationships with suppliers. To keep those relationships sound, we meet with all major suppliers (there are now 120) once each year. In addition, we send the president of each supplier company a quarterly update on the quality of the parts that company makes.

Management on the Spot

After nearly two years of work, the first company-wide Quality Team assessed its accomplishments before turning its work over to the second team in 1982. The team's report wàs sobering for all of us, especially the managers. This is what it said:

Although we feel that the first round of the Quality Process was valuable and, in some areas, successful, the most recurring theme coming from our critique is the lack of integration and consistency.

Some of the unevenness in the program's implementation was due to inadequate training and communication by the Quality Team, but much of it was due to untrained or insensitive managers.

We feel that the greatest potential obstacle to future progress in the Quality Process will be ineffective managers:

- *Managers who do not know how to get their people involved in problem solving and decision making.*
- *Managers who do not know how to develop their people into highly skilled workers and leaders.*
- *Managers who do not know how to teach by example.*
- *Managers who do not know how to develop an organizational climate which is conducive to solving problems and generating high performance.*
- *Managers who rely on the old adversarial and autocratic management styles that are foreign to a quality-oriented company.*
- *Managers who don't know how to listen.*

Obviously, we were not communicating as well as we thought at Tennant Company. The team recommended an intensive program of management training with a focus on people skills and the principles of participative management. "Only when we have consistently effective people managers will we have a truly successful Quality Process and a dynamic organization," the team's report concluded.

The second Quality Team chose to begin by working on listening— mainly because it seemed the basis for all other communication skills. We called on Sperry Corporation to teach our trainers the listening skills program it had used. Over a year's time, all of our supervisors and managers took a listening course. After learning the techniques of good listening, we began working on verbal communications skills. And about the time the managers and supervisors completed their training in effective communication, small groups were beginning to form to work on specific problems. So we

"We feel that the greatest potential obstacle to future progress in the Quality Process will be ineffective managers." Quality Team I.

began learning about group dynamics and how groups can work effectively together—a process that continues today at Tennant Company.

Recognizing Quality

The successes we achieved in our pilot programs and the small groups that began springing up throughout the company to work on quality problems were encouraging signs that quality was being taken seriously. Our next challenge was to find a way to reward people who were making exceptional contributions toward our efforts.

Our first step was to set up a formal awards program with award recipients nominated by their peers (see appendix for Quality Recognition nomination form). We created group as well as individual awards, because some of the most striking examples of quality improvement at our company are the result of teamwork.

Individual awards are given to no more than 2 percent of our work

41

force during any one year. The highest individual award is the Award of Excellence, symbolized by a specially designed gold and diamond ring that is presented at a dinner attended by the award winners, the management committee (including the president), and the award-winners' guests. Special Recognition awards are given to a select number of individuals who are nominated but who are not Award of Excellence recipients. Those awards are symbolized by a pin and plaque.

> **"Recognizing employees' contributions toward quality has to be more than a once- or twice-a-year affair."**
> **Quality Team I.**

The Group Excellence Awards are given twice a year in two categories—one for permanent and one for temporary work groups—with no more than six awards made each time.

We realized that recognizing employees' contributions toward quality has to be more than a once- or twice-a-year affair. So we formed a positive feedback committee to encourage daily recognition throughout the company. The committee recommended training for managers and supervisors in how to give positive reinforcement to people who have done an especially good job. Additional recognition programs have been added as we have seen the need for them. In 1983, another group, called Quality Special Projects, created the Koala T. Bear award, an informal recognition program in which once a month, a member of the group dons the company's Koala T. Bear suit and goes to the employee's office or station to present the award. Recipients are consistent quality performers nominated by the peers or by supervisors or managers (see appendix for Koala T. Bear award nomination form).

Tennant Company also has a system of financial rewards for improvement suggestions made by employees. For many years (it began in the mid-1940s), the suggestion program applied only to individuals. If a person turned in a suggestion and it was adopted, that person would receive 20 percent of the first year's savings (after implementation costs) related to the suggestion.

We saw, however, that a suggestion made by one person, for which he or she was rewarded, could produce unwelcome change for co-workers and cause resentment. In 1982, to reduce the risk of individual suggestions backfiring, we expanded the program to include rewards for suggestions made by employee groups. Group awards provide financial incentives for increasing efficiency and productivity, and many of the small groups formed to work on particular problems have used the suggestion program to net rewards for themselves as well as substantial savings for the company.

Spinning Out

A number of additional projects have emerged at Tennant Company as part of—or as the result of—the quality emphasis. The application of JIT (Just-In-Time) manufacturing is a good example.

JIT manufacturing enables Tennant Company to operate with a very short supply of assembly components. Ideally, a company making the best use of JIT manufacturing would have on hand only the parts needed to manufacture one day's products. The purpose is to reduce the need for physical expansion and to make better use of space—one of the highest costs in any business. Tennant Company began planning for JIT in 1981 when a critical shortage of storage space became apparent. For five months, a manufacturing group met weekly to develop alternatives to building additional space. Their ideas included reducing production set-ups, minimizing assembly lots, JIT delivery from sub-contractors and vendors, overlapping production operations, preventive maintenance systems, executing an exact planned production schedule, and synchronizing the flow system that controls manufacturing operations.

Implementing these steps began with training 50 production and department managers in JIT manufacturing principles. The first application began in 1983, when one of our managers noticed 100 engines in the stockroom waiting to be installed in machines not yet in production. Noting that each machine-sized space carried an annual cost of $175, he quickly calculated the tremendous cost of maintaining such an inventory. He formed a small group to do cost/benefit analyses of three different manufacturing methods, including JIT. They concluded that JIT was the most productive and profitable method, even though it would challenge a company whose products include numerous customer-chosen options. (There are more than a million variations possible in current Tennant Company standard bills of material.)

JIT requires good communication and cooperation both within the company and with vendors. At Tennant Company, we have been able to improve communication significantly. Work groups cooperate so the manufacturing flow is continuous. For example, in manufacturing our Model 432, the welding department welds four frames a day, the paint department paints four, and assembly puts together four, all in a circle. No part is made and sent to the stockroom, so extra steps and time are saved as well as inventory and storage space.

The Ripple Effect

Quality affects other programs within a company. It took us a long time to understand how that happens, but we have proof that it does. For example, quality affects safety—an important concern for Tennant Company, as it is for most manufacturers.

For years, the major focus of our safety program has been to reduce the number of accidents that cause workers lost time on the job. We do that in a number of ways, including paying constant attention to the cleanliness of our plants.

The quality process has helped us make our plants even cleaner. Employees have become committed to a quality environment, and thanks to them, our factories have become the showcase of our industry.

Our safety achievements have been equally dramatic. Part of my job in the past was working with managers to set goals for reducing lost-time accidents. Today, we have plants that have gone six years without a single lost-time accident. Now we work on goals to reduce the number of minor injuries that require first-aid attention of a nurse or physician. **R.K.**

The quality emphasis and the study of JIT manufacturing also led to the development of work cells in manufacturing and assembly. In a work cell, all the steps required to manufacture a specific part are done in one area. Early in the quality process, a group of people in the machine shop began looking for a way to reduce set-up and through-put time—the time it takes a part to go through all operations in the factory. First, a group of industrial engineers, supervisors, and employees (the Process Operations Committee) studied the processes and operations in the sheet metal area and in the machine shop. They analyzed 50,000 operations in machine shop and sheet metal and diagrammed exactly how raw material was transformed into piece parts as material flowed through various work centers and departments (see Figure 1, page 46).

The diagram showed the group members how to organize work and move machines to manage the process more efficiently. In one area, they moved a press brake, a rod parting machine, a drill press, a small turret lathe, and a chamfer machine to a common work area—the "480 work cell" (see Figure 2, page 46).

This area processes all one-inch diameter and smaller round stock. A typical part is cut, threaded, drilled, and formed in this single work cell. Raw steel is stored in the area, so operators can pull their material from stock as they need it. This not only reduces inventory costs but allows operators to produce a part from start to finish all in one work area. The lead time needed to send a part through several work areas is eliminated. As a result, the eight-day average for parts fabrication has been reduced to a single day.

A second work cell was organized after the Process Operations Committee study was analyzed to see what processes were being duplicated in work areas besides the machine shop. It was discovered that a number of operations were being duplicated in the sheet metal area, and that many could be consolidated for greater efficiency. Because of this finding, "work cell 108" was organized in January 1986. All bar stock is processed—cut, punched, drilled, and formed—in this work cell. (See Figures 3 and 4, page 48, for "before" and "after" diagrams of sheet metal work flow.) All operations done on a particular part are performed in one area, making it possible to complete the operation in minutes or hours instead of days.

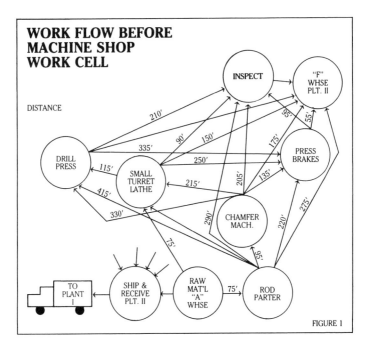

WORK FLOW BEFORE MACHINE SHOP WORK CELL

DISTANCE

FIGURE 1

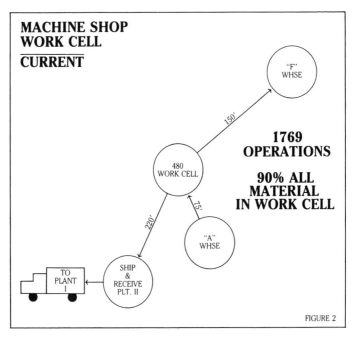

MACHINE SHOP WORK CELL

CURRENT

1769 OPERATIONS

90% ALL MATERIAL IN WORK CELL

FIGURE 2

An important benefit of the work cell is the cross training that employees receive. People who once specialized in one operation now know five or six functions because, as a part of the work cell, they rotate operations and learn each other's jobs. Another benefit is the ability the employees now have to plan their work schedules according to what needs to be done. In addition, if a mistake is made, parts can be reworked immediately, saving time previously spent routing a part to rework.

The work cells are a dramatic change for employees. And even when it makes a big difference in efficiency, change is not automatically accepted. At Tennant Company, the work had been done the same way for more than 30 years. At first, the changes were resisted. But gradually, people became enthusiastic. Suggestions began to pour in. Hundreds of hours of operations time were cut because of suggestions by employees, and thousands of dollars were saved.

Another company-wide project that is also related to quality is education in Value Analysis, a method of eliminating any factor that contributes to cost but not to worth or function. An interdepartmental group used Value Analysis techniques to refine international shipping procedures and reduce the number of days needed to ship international rush orders. This team was made up of representatives from the international department, shipping/receiving, and productivity improvement. The group's efforts resulted in reducing the number of days to ship rush orders overseas from nine to two working days for 97 percent of the orders received. The group estimated its work would save Tennant Company $15,500 and 1,920 hours of labor every year.

This is just a sample of the many small-group projects that have spun out of our quality emphasis. At last count, we could name 80 projects, not including short-term activities generated by specific work groups. Their names range from no-nonsense descriptions (Torque Control Team) to imaginative acronyms such as TEME 5 (Tennant Explosion in Manufacturing Excellence); TIP (Tennant Improvement on Productivity); RISLIP (Reduce Inventory, Space, Labor, Improve Productivity); and PEPPER (Pension, Payroll, Personnel). They have focused on specific manufacturing problems (Pyroform Brush Tubes Committee), new ways of working together (Mixed Model Build Group, Model 480 Work Cell Group), company-wide issues (Ad Hoc Disability Management Group,

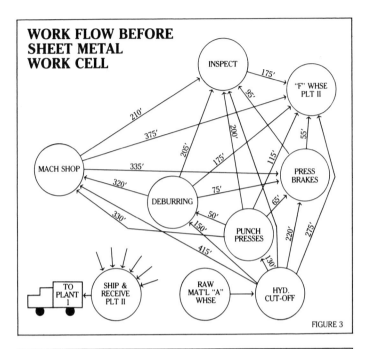

WORK FLOW BEFORE SHEET METAL WORK CELL

INSPECT

"F" WHSE PLT II

175'

95'

210'

375'

205'

200'

175'

115'

55'

MACH SHOP

335'

PRESS BRAKES

320'

75'

65'

DEBURRING

50'

330'

150'

PUNCH PRESSES

220'

275'

415'

130'

TO PLANT 1

SHIP & RECEIVE PLT II

RAW MAT'L "A" WHSE

HYD. CUT-OFF

FIGURE 3

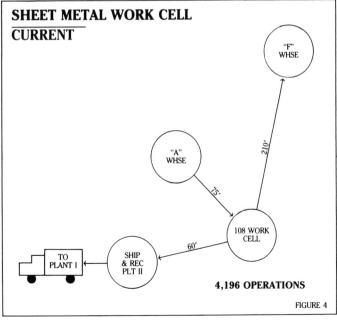

SHEET METAL WORK CELL
CURRENT

"F" WHSE

"A" WHSE

210'

75'

108 WORK CELL

60'

TO PLANT 1

SHIP & REC PLT II

4,196 OPERATIONS

FIGURE 4

Name Tag Awareness Group), or new product development (the Mustang Team, the Filly Team). All have been generated by the employees who are directly involved in the work. At the most recent Zero Defects Day in 1985, 41 of those groups created displays to demonstrate their accomplishments.

The Sales Force—Quality Eyes and Ears

Tennant Company's direct sales force plays a critical role in the quality process. Our sales people have made it their responsibility to see that zero-defects machines are delivered to our customers. Every time a machine is delivered, the salesperson fills out an installation report. If there are defects, each one is the subject of a separate report. The reports are sent to the warranty and quality departments at company headquarters. In 1979, when the quality emphasis began, 13 percent of the machines we sold showed at least one defect at installation. By 1983, cooperation between sales and manufacturing had reduced the rate of defects at installation to 6.2 percent.

The sales reps found that zero-defects principles could be applied to their work as well as to manufacturing. Here's an example: Demonstrations of TENNANT machines are a significant part of sales activity. They require time and coordination. The sales person has a machine shipped to the customer's site, and a demonstration driver arrives to show what the machine can do. If the right customer isn't there, time and money are wasted, and the sales person must reschedule for another time.

The New York district sales force developed a plan to reduce unnecessary repeat demonstrations to potential customers. They saw that many of those repeats were due to errors on the sales representative's part—not contacting the right people for the first demonstration and not confirming appointments. They calculated the cost to the company in the sales representative's time, as well as the demonstration driver's time and gas. By contacting the right people and confirming appointments, the New York sales people reduced the number of repeat demonstrations from 8 per month at the beginning of 1982 to 1.5 per month at year-end, at a savings of approximately $600 to $1,000 per demonstration.

Focusing on Warranties

By 1983, we were feeling confident enough in our quality process to make some bold declarations about our products. We formed a Product Reliability Committee and charged it with the responsibility of meeting these objectives: 1) to decrease the cost of warranties as a percentage of sales while increasing customer satisfaction throughout the life of the product, 2) to address reliability problems that cause customer dissatisfaction, and 3) to extend warranty coverage on new and current products without increased cost to Tennant Company or its customers.

One of the boldest measures of our confidence was our decision in 1982 to announce the industry's first two-year or 2,000-hour limited warranty on a sweeper—along with guaranteed credit when the machine was traded in on a newer model. We could offer these industry firsts because we had achieved better machine design, durability, and performance. These achievements resulted mainly from our efforts to improve quality.

In May 1983, we staged our second Zero Defects Day. It began with a review of the quality process at company headquarters and plant tours for public officials and people from other companies as well as for Tennant Company employees. Later in the day, on the stage of the Guthrie Theater in Minneapolis, 1,000 employees watched a team of co-workers dramatize the impact of doing things right the first time. This time we had the attention of the local media, including on-the-spot coverage by two local television news teams.

By 1984, we had evidence that just about everyone in the company was thinking about quality, and that many efforts to improve were being made every day. Here's an example: In the past, employees in the field warehouses routinely ran out of shipping forms, causing shipping to come to a halt until more forms arrived by air from the central warehouse. Central warehouse employees began to look for ways to improve. Now, they check with the field warehouses at the beginning of each month and send out an additional supply of forms if needed. The warehouse personnel do not run out of forms, shipping operations continue without interruption, the company saves time, and it saves the money previously spent shipping the forms by air-freight.

Another example is what we call the "green box high-rise project" that condensed parts storage from 1,300 square feet of racking to a mere 288 square feet. Previously, drawer-like bins were stored on separate pallets, four to six per pallet. A group of people from material handling and shipping/receiving brainstormed creative alternatives and came up with a simple but effective way of saving space. They rearranged the parts in front-access boxes stacked in "high-rise" racks. Not only did the new arrangement cut down on storage space (savings were calculated at $27,781 per year), it also increased the ability to remove needed parts more quickly and safely. As a result, inventory accuracy increased to 98 percent.

Quality-focused projects were occurring not only in Minneapolis but in every Tennant Company location. Our British subsidiary, Tennant Maintenance Systems, has programs in place to increase the number of orders that can be shipped complete, reduce back orders, improve service calls, and ensure quality application of TENNANT floor coatings. The Atlanta regional office has a team working on reducing paper errors. The New York sales force asked its service representatives to help generate leads as part of the service force's quality goals. As a result, service representatives generated 51 new leads within one year. Small but vital signs like these tell us that quality is becoming part of the woodwork at Tennant Company.

However, just knowing that people are paying attention isn't enough. One of the most important elements of our quality emphasis is reducing the cost of not doing things right the first time. By the end of 1985, we had reduced the cost of quality (all costs associated with not doing things right the first time, including the costs of prevention, appraisal, and failure) from 17 percent in 1980 to 7.9 percent of sales (see Figure 5, page 54). More specific results include:

- Defects in machines received by customers have been reduced by 63 percent.
- Defects discovered prior to shipping have been reduced by 52 percent.
- Warranty/scrap and rework expense had dropped from 1.62 percent of sales in 1981 to 1.15 percent in 1986.
- Quality problems at installation of our machines have fallen from

13 percent of machines shipped in 1979 to 5.6 percent in 1985.

- Manufacturing rework hours have been reduced from 33,900 hours in 1980 to 6,800 hours in 1986.
- The reject rate for parts purchased from our suppliers has fallen from 6.8 percent in 1980 to 1.7 percent in 1986, and our suppliers have reduced defects in the components they provide for us by 59 percent.

WARRANTY, SCRAP, AND REWORK EXPENSE AS A PERCENT OF SALES

PERCENT

| 1.62% | 1.58% | 1.37% | 1.29% | 1.29% | 1.15% |

1981 1982 1983 1984 1985 1986

- The percentage of orders shipped within 24 hours of receipt has increased from 47 percent in 1980 to more than 75 percent.
- The percentage of machines arriving undamaged in transit has increased from 94.7 percent in 1980 to 97.8 percent in mid-1985.

By our third Zero Defects Day, we had reached a new stage in our journey. For six years, we had concentrated on doing things right. Now, we were turning our attention to making sure we were doing the right things.

In terms of Phil Crosby's Quality Maturity Grid, our company has progressed from "Stage I: Uncertainty," where we were in 1979, to "Stage IV: Wisdom," which we reached last year (see Quality Maturity Grid, page 56). We're not quite ready for "Certainty," but we hope to achieve it eventually.

In the following pages, you will find brief discussions of some of the lessons we've learned so far. But one of the most important lessons is unwritten: The quest for quality never ends. A company can make progress, and even reach the point where it has no quality problems. But unless quality improvement is a continual activity, all the progress that has been made will be lost. If we can help it, that will not happen at Tennant Company.

COST OF QUALITY

1980
17% OF SALES

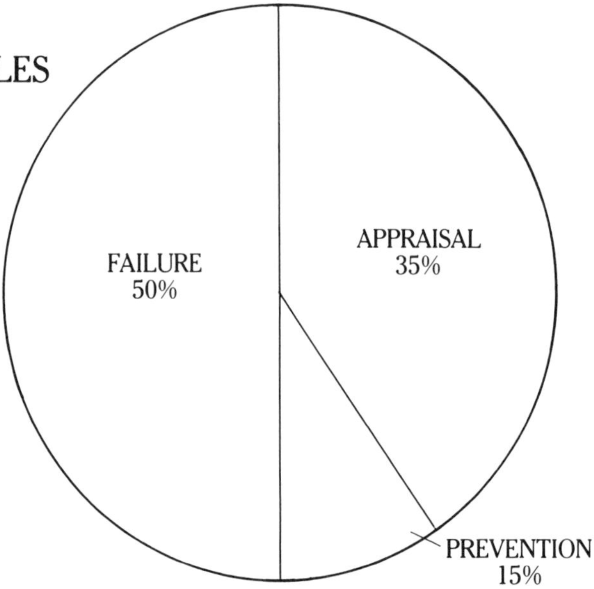

FAILURE
50%

APPRAISAL
35%

PREVENTION
15%

1986 THROUGH MAY
7.9% OF SALES

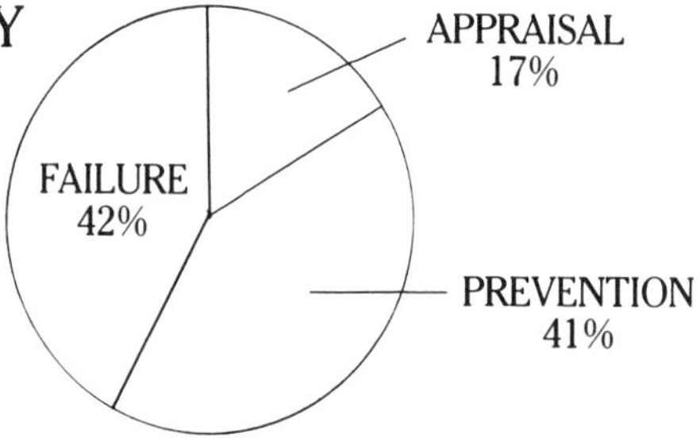

APPRAISAL
17%

FAILURE
42%

PREVENTION
41%

1988
2.5% OF SALES

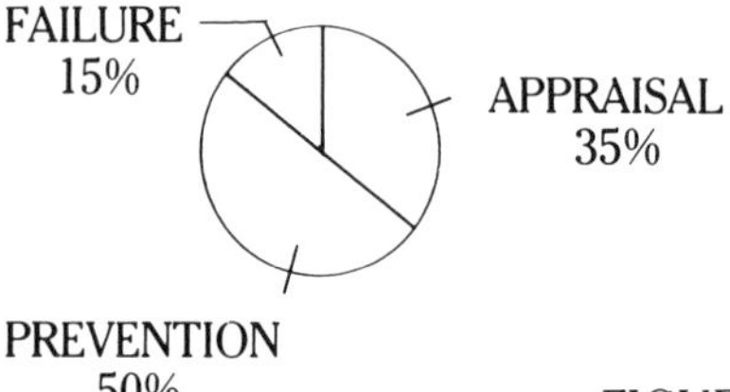

FAILURE
15%

APPRAISAL
35%

PREVENTION
50%

FIGURE 5

The Cost of Doing Things Wrong

Determining just how much it costs to do things wrong is a difficult process. At Tennant Company, there are actually three types of costs.

Failure costs. These costs fall into two categories:

1. *Internal failure costs* include money spent correcting errors and redoing tasks that were not done right the first time. At our company, good examples of internal failure costs are rework, scrap, and computer reruns.

2. *External failure costs* include money lost because customers were dissatisfied with the product or service they received. It costs us a lot of money to deliver products that do not conform to requirements. An example of these costs is money spent on warranties.

Appraisal costs. These include money spent on inspecting and checking to detect things that were done wrong. Tennant Company examples include part inspection, final product tests, other quality checks, drafting checks, and computer program testing.

Prevention costs. These include funds spent to make sure things are done right. Training and planning are good examples, as are supplier qualification programs, Quality Team meetings, new product design reviews, and preventive maintenance.

Appraisal and prevention are considered costs of quality because if we were all doing our jobs right the first time, we wouldn't need inspection or prevention. But we live in an imperfect and constantly changing world, and we know that a certain amount of attention must continually be paid to doing things right the first time, as well as reviewing requirements to be sure they are proper and current.

If we have to spend money on quality, it's obvious to us that of the three types of cost—failure, appraisal, and prevention—we have been spending too much money on failure and appraisal and not enough on prevention. **R.K.**

QUALITY MANAGEMENT MATURITY GRID
Rater: Hale/Hoelscher/Kowal

Measurement Categories	Stage I: Uncertainty (1979)	Stage II: Awakening (1980)	
Management understanding and attitude	No comprehension of quality as a management tool. Tend to blame quality department for "quality problems."	Recognizing that quality management may be of value, but not willing to provide money or time to make it all happen.	
Quality organization status	Quality is hidden in manufacturing or engineering departments. Inspection probably not part of organization. Emphasis on appraisal and sorting.	A stronger quality leader is appointed, but main emphasis is still on appraisal and moving the product. Still part of manufacturing or other.	
Problem handling	Problems are fought as they occur; no resolution; inadequate definition; lots of yelling and accusations.	Teams are set up to attack major problems. Long-range solutions are not solicited.	
Cost of quality as % of sales	Reported: unknown Actual: 20%	Reported: 3% Actual: 18%	
Quality improvement actions	No organized activities. No understanding of such activities.	Trying obvious "motivational" short-range efforts.	
Summation of company quality posture	"We don't know why we have problems with quality."	"Is it absolutely necessary to always have problems with quality?"	

Unit: **Tennant Company**		
Stage III: (1983) Enlightenment	**Stage IV: Wisdom (1986)**	**Stage V: Certainty**
While going through quality improvement program, learn more about quality management, becoming more supportive and helpful.	Participating. Understand absolutes of quality management. Recognize their personal role in continuing emphasis.	Consider quality management as essential part of company system.
Quality department reports to top management, all appraisal is incorporated and manager has role in management of company.	Quality manager is an officer of company, effective status reporting and preventive action. Involved with consumer affairs and special assignments.	Quality manager on board of directors. Prevention is main concern. Quality is a thought leader.
Corrective action communication established. Problems are faced openly and resolved in an orderly way.	Problems are identified early in their development. All functions are open to suggestion and improvement.	Except in the most unusual cases, problems are prevented.
Reported: 8% Actual: 12%	Reported: 6.5% Actual: 8%	Reported: 2.5% Actual: 2.5%
Implementation of the 14-step program with thorough understanding and establishment of each step.	Continuing the 14-step program and starting Make Certain.	Quality improvement is a normal and continued activity.
"Through management commitment and quality improvement, we are identifying and resolving our problems."	"Defect prevention is a routine part of our operation."	"We know why we do not have problems with quality."

TWO

THE FIVE MOST IMPORTANT FACTORS FOR SUCCESS

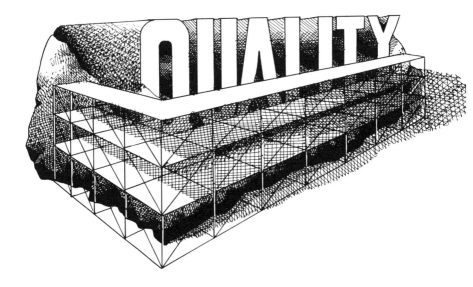

THE FIVE MOST IMPORTANT FACTORS FOR SUCCESS

The how-tos of quality are not difficult to master. For any company seeking to implement a quality emphasis, there is plenty of help available through consultants, books, and manuals of many kinds. You can learn to measure the cost of quality, read the books and manuals, form small groups or quality circles, and do all of the other activities that are part of a quality emphasis. But unless five critical factors are present in your company, you will not achieve lasting improvement in quality. Here are the factors we believe are absolutely necessary for success:

1. Management commitment
2. Employee involvement
3. Cooperative, non-adversarial worker/manager relationships
4. Rewards for the people
5. Time, energy, and determination

Management Commitment: Start at the Top

The foundation that is the basis for building a tradition of quality and the strengths that flow through zero-defects concepts derive from one fundamental source—genuine and uncompromising commitment to quality by everyone, especially top management.

Vince Lombardi once said, "Winning isn't everything; it's the only thing." Six years into our quality journey, we're convinced that like winning, quality has to be the only thing—or at least first among equals, the equals being costs and schedules.

Making quality first among equals requires company-wide commitment, especially the commitment of every member of the management team. Commitment is more than a verbal agreement to a program or a process. It means more that merely setting aside time and money for training and planning, although both are essential. Commitment means full participation—time, budget, and personal involvement.

Commitment must start at the top of the organization, with the company's leaders. When the CEO publicly takes a firm stand for quality, the message is clear. And when the CEO's commitment is communicated to the next management level, chances are increased that those managers will participate.

Committed managers don't develop overnight, however. A company's executives are like any other group when it comes to new ideas—a mixture of believers, nonbelievers, and downright skeptics. So it probably won't surprise you to learn that Tennant Company had its share of skeptics.

Some of our executives were skeptical because they misunderstood the fundamental nature of what we were doing. No matter how we tried to show that quality was concrete and measurable—the result of doing things right the first time—some of our managers continued to think of our efforts as a motivational program. They saw the banners and the pledges, the enthusiasm of ZD Day—and waited for the excitement to blow over. They were unconvinced, and they stayed unconvinced for a long time.

Commitment means full participation— time, budget, and personal involvement.

Even when they agreed to support our efforts, these executives remained uncommitted. Because they were skeptical, they sent out mixed signals to their employees. If a choice had to be made between a quality-related meeting and one for new product development, for example, product development won out. Quality was seen as "soft" —no matter how "hard" the cost-of-quality numbers appeared to be.

Living with a few skeptics is easy when overall enthusiasm is high. But improving quality can be tedious, even boring at times, and enthusiasm wanes. When that happens, the skeptics' views can be destructive. It's important to find the key to their interest and, finally, their commitment.

At Tennant Company, that key turned out to be our executive incentive program. A portion of each executive's compensation is tied to the achievement of personal work goals established in consultation with our company's president. For example, some of Doug's 1985-86 quality-related goals as vice president for engineering, manufacturing, and purchasing included, among others, the following:

- meet Tennant Company's 1986 warranty goals
- meet Tennant Company's 1986 cost of quality goals
- meet Tennant Company's 1986 machine installation goals
- develop a process for setting specific goals, small group activity, regular reviews, and top-level involvement by April 30, 1985
- conduct a worldwide study of Tennant Company's commitment to meeting customer needs *as viewed by the customer*. Recommend necessary changes by December 31, 1985.

If those goals had not been met, Doug's compensation would have been adjusted downward.

Now, each Tennant Company executive is asked to make at least one quality-related goal, and that goal is weighted against the compensation the executive receives. With compensation riding on achievement of that goal, there is a personal reason to become involved. Once involved, the skeptics invariably become believers.

Converting skeptical managers, however, can be especially difficult in non-manufacturing areas. Consider, for example, a vice president of marketing whose response at the beginning of the quality effort was "Great, manufacturing and quality control are finally waking up." For him, quality meant not having the rear wheel on a TENNANT sweeper fall off as the machine was being uncrated for the customer. Or a machine *not* blowing a seal after eight hours of operation. Headaches like those represented quality—or lack of it—to sales people and marketing managers.

According to Phil Crosby, quality applies to everybody. Says the marketing VP, "When we heard Crosby, we nodded our heads, but we really believed that quality was mainly the factory's job."

When the second Quality Team was formed in 1982, it included several volunteers from the marketing vice president's area. He was only slightly embarrassed when, at the end of a year, they had nothing to report from marketing—no progress, no involvement.

Then in 1983, he began to see more complaints from customers—not about the machines they were purchasing, but about sales and field service. Sales people weren't returning customers' calls. Invoices were riddled with mistakes. Repair bills were skyrocketing. Maybe, he thought, Crosby had something after all.

In January 1983, the marketing VP gave himself and his division nine months to improve their work. Taking their cues from manufacturing, they began measuring the cost of quality to their areas. Sales office staff counted the number of times price quotations had to be re-done because of mistakes. Sales people recorded the number of no-contact calls. Office walls were covered with bar graphs and charts.

Six months later, the charts showed no substantial improvement.

Measurement alone wasn't working, the VP concluded, and he called his managers together. "Let's stop counting mistakes and do something meaningful," he told them. They created small groups to work on specific problems. For example, the sales training group wanted to find out if quality-related tools such as brainstorming, graphing, and pareto diagramming could be applied to sales training. They tested the tools with the Minnesota district and eventually incorporated some of them into field sales training. Their progress was recorded in minutes of the meetings.

Gradually, enthusiasm began to build. By the end of the next year, half the Award of Excellence recipients were from this vice president's area. The year before retirement, one of his quality goals was to attend every major meeting about quality in the marketing division, from Atlanta to Anaheim. He retired with the conviction that attention to quality pays off when the right approach is found and when management is truly committed to making it work.

The Champions

Maintaining a steady, consistent quality effort would be difficult in a company that has frequent management changes. At Tennant Company, we're lucky to have managers and executives who have been around for a long time. They recognize that zero defects won't be achieved in one year, or six years, or maybe even ten. They've learned to recognize progress in small but incremental gains, and they're going to be with the company long enough to see how it turns out. So they support the quality process with time, funding, and personal involvement.

But even when management as a whole backs a quality emphasis and is willing to commit both time and budget, efforts to make changes can die of inertia when obstacles arise. Chances for success are increased if there is at least one champion for quality among top management. That champion must be a person willing to take risks, cut through red tape, and commit dollars to quality improvement projects.

Champions are managers who see that the funds are there when improvements need to be made. They act as mentors to small groups working on specific problems. Because they have the power to overcome organizational barriers, they often make the difference in helping a group accomplish its objectives. In our company, these champions make time to be continually involved in one or two small groups. Because many are upper-level managers, there is the added benefit of increased understanding of management among line employees.

These champions regularly set aside time for quality-related projects and set specific quarterly and yearly goals related to the quality emphasis. The vice president for manufacturing and engineering (Doug) commits four hours each week to working with small groups as a mentor

Doing a Little Extra

Frank Smith is a good example of an employee who takes quality seriously. Frank is one of the people responsible for making sure the Tennant Company factory has the reputation of being one of the cleanest in the country. A painter in the maintenance department, he has been painting interior and exterior walls and ceilings at Tennant Company for years. Frank has applied hundreds of gallons of white paint each year at the request of department managers, who remember once in a while to thank him for the good job. Nevertheless, Frank knew he was doing an important job. And there is no doubt in our minds that a clean plant is one of the highest priority objectives in any quality process. When people take pride in their work areas, they will also take pride in their work.

About six years ago, as part of the quality emphasis, Frank decided to put a little extra into his job. He began creating wall murals—pictures of fish, grouse, or deer, paintings of Tennant Company products, slogans about Quality, or whatever the people who work in the area requested. Every year, requests for his work increase, along with the positive comments on what a great job he is doing. Frank proves that quality can be achieved in more ways than in assembling products. He achieves quality with a brush, ladder, a bucket of paint, and a fertile imagination. **R.K.**

and troubleshooter. The director of manufacturing (Ron) spends a large percentage of his time on the factory floor, providing support and positive reinforcement to small groups working on specific problems.

Champions can also come from the ranks of the hourly workers. A welder who became involved in one of the first quality small groups in his department became its informal leader. Then he volunteered for the second company-wide Quality Team. From there he went to the Zero Defects Day planning committee. As he learned more and did more, he became an articulate spokesman for quality within the company. In 1983, he and his co-workers were asked to make a presentation at the Tennant-Company-sponsored Japan Management Association meeting. Now, this former welder is a supervisor—and a champion for quality company-wide.

Tennant Company demonstrates its commitment to quality by allocating personnel and financial resources to the many programs within the quality emphasis. The company's director of manufacturing engineering and product conformance is an advisor for every two-year Quality Team, and he devotes 20 percent of his time to the team's efforts. Funding is reserved for training and recognition programs. When budgets must be trimmed, those funds remain. In other words, management is willing to pay the price—in money and time—to make the quality process an integral part of the company's culture.

Employee Involvement: 30 Percent at a Time

Quality is built upon a framework of common purposes. Management and employees share the same objective: Do it right the first time.

Even when every member of the management group is 100 percent committed to quality, very little will happen if employees are uninterested or uninvolved. Employees can be just as skeptical as managers, sometimes even more so, especially when they're asked to change the way they work.

We approached the job of involving our work force by setting both long- and short-range goals for bringing employees into the process. In the first two years, we decided, if we can get 30 percent of the people involved in zero defects and quality, we'll be happy. As it turned out, about 30 percent did participate during the first two years. And almost 100 percent signed the first quality pledge that first ZD Day. So we set our sights on bringing in the next 30 percent in two more years. Again, we achieved our goal. By now, we believe that 90 percent of the people who work at Tennant Company have been involved in the quality effort in one way or another, and we're quite satisfied. We recognize that there will always be some who aren't interested, and that's their choice.

When we say that 90 percent of our people are involved in the quality effort, we mean that they use quality-related principles to do their jobs. Not all of that 90 percent have been part of small groups. Some prefer to quietly apply the principles to their work, setting and meeting personal goals.

Although we insist on technically accurate measurements to gauge our progress in every other area, our calculation of the number of people involved throughout the company is made purely by "gut feel." A manager who spends the time he or she should on the floor, close to where the work is done, will know. We have a number of informal indicators that tell us quickly the level of quality in various parts of the company. One such indicator is a member of the welding department, one of the most accomplished welders who has ever worked at Tennant Company. His work is perfection, and his standards are high. When this welder isn't complaining, we know that the parts coming from the fabrication departments are good, and we know that quality is on the minds of the people who make them.

Some employees, like this welder, have never served on a Quality Team or small group. But they know quality when they see it; when they don't see it, we know we have to find out why.

How did we enlist 90 percent of our people in this effort to build quality into our culture? It didn't happen automatically. First, the managers had to become involved. Then they asked others to join them, and recognized them for jobs well done. Soon, traditional barriers between management and employees began breaking down, and the people on the floor began to see that their jobs would be made easier and more interesting if they took part.

Some employees have never served on a quality team or in a small group, but they know quality when they see it; when they don't see it, we have to find out why.

One employee in the machine shop explains. "There are a lot of programs that come and go. But this one was done on such a broad scale. Almost every person at Tennant Company was involved; it wasn't only the people out on the floor. It became clear that everyone has to be involved in the quality program and do his or her part to maintain that high level of quality."

In the past, we hired people to do their jobs and nothing else. In fact, we frowned on any activity *except* the job. We didn't ask production employees to help design new products or improve procedures. But the quality emphasis gave us an opportunity to tap the knowledge and skill the people who do the production work. We could ask them to help us achieve our goals by becoming involved.

It wasn't easy, at first, because we were all learning to work together in small groups. In many ways, first-line supervisors found it the most difficult. Quality groups made changes in their work patterns and time-tested ways of doing things. Some supervisors felt threatened by the involvement of the people they supervised. But after two years of training in group process skills, supervisors have the confidence they need to help their work groups function as a real team.

Now we have two major challenges: to introduce new employees to our quality process, and to keep enthusiasm for quality projects alive.

In Their Own Words: Tennant Company Employees

Conrad Hoffman has a particular definition of the word "junk": products that meet specifications but are nonfunctional. Hoffman says, "I believe we have to build a product that does what the customers expect at an affordable price, yet allows Tennant Company to make a profit." Hoffman is a final test inspector in the assembly area. He and his colleagues are the last people to see TENNANT machines before they are shipped. For them, the quality emphasis means making sure the machines are shipped defect free. "The best part of my job comes from watching a perfect final product leave our hands. It's especially rewarding to hear good reports from customers."

"There's nothing like the feeling of accomplishment when we produce a good product. It all boils down to producing a quality product, the best way." **Ray Korus**, brush department manager.

Tennant Company's technical publications department produces all the manuals that customers receive with TENNANT machines, plus instruction bulletins for service, repair, and replacement kits. The manuals include parts numbers and serial numbers, plus drawings of parts so the customer and service representative can identify them more easily. "Tech Pub," as it is called, is a key department in customer service. The department has its own in-house typesetting equipment and stat camera, so revisions can be done easily and deadlines met. Says supervisor **Randy Sauer**, "We believe our work is an extremely visible reflection of our company, since our manuals are tools for sales, service, and public relations."

"All of us have been concentrating for six years on *doing things right*. We're at a plateau now, and ready to move to higher ground, to think about *doing the right things*. In my own work, I write reports, I conduct meetings, I meet people, I give speeches. I hope I do those things right, and I hope I'm making progress to a goal of zero defects. But now I must ask myself: "Are these the right meetings? The right speeches? Am I meeting with the right people? Am I doing the right things, as well as doing them right?" **Roger Hale**, at ZD Day 1985.

"Quality is a policy, a process, and an internal belief and attitude. Before the first ZD Day showed that the whole company was behind quality, we tried to implement programs in individual departments. Enthusiasm didn't last because not everyone was involved.

People know that the quality process is here to stay because it hasn't changed or waned. Now, when they see potential problems, they say something about them. Quality groups work on problems in their areas, to make the product better and the work safer. Management trusts employees' ability to solve problems, and is confident enough to let go." **Jan Lund**, shop floor control.

"We have learned that quality is more than making sure nuts and bolts are tightened to the right specifications. When we first started, quality was defined by everyone in a different way. It was never stated in terms of business profits, growth, or opportunity. Now we are expanding the concept of quality to mean a growing, profitable, opportunistic business. Now, in addition to doing things right for our customers, we're also focusing on internal relationships. We're concentrating on making sure that each department in the company understands the requirements of the others." **Barry Fisher**, marketing.

"Americans expect instant results. But changing a company's culture takes a long time. The key is to make sure management really understands what is being done and is committed to it. Without management's understanding and commitment, employees don't have an example to follow." **Bill Strang**, international marketing.

"The quality process can do nothing but help us. It will help expand our business, which in turn will mean greater profitability for the company, which will mean greater job security and greater opportunity for advancement for each employee." **Pat Johnson**, training.

At Tennant Company, our concern with quality is hard to miss because the company's commitment has neither changed nor waned. New employees see that we don't expect them to shrug off production or communications problems. Quality is *everyone's* job. There's a sense of enthusiasm that comes from accomplishment, and confidence that the methods and tools we've learned do work. All across the company, small groups are making our products better and the work safer. Many of these groups have formed without the knowledge or involvement of top management. Change has occurred, not only in the manufacturing processes, but in the belief system of the company.

Cooperative, Non-adversarial Worker/ Management Relationships

The quality environment offers an employee an opportunity to participate in a shared objective. It offers membership in a team effort. It extends the comforts of working and building together—instead of against each other.

It may seem unusual for a manufacturing company working on productivity to be concerned with the idea of cooperation. But when an organization attempts to make permanent cultural changes, cooperation is essential. And cooperation implies a non-adversarial atmosphere, where working together is the accepted way of getting the work done.

The principles seem so elementary. Cooperation occurs when everyone is working toward a common goal. Unfortunately, the structure of many American businesses does not lend itself to cooperation. There are many barriers between management and workers, and sometimes those barriers develop into adversarial relationships. When that happens, workers distrust management and management distrusts workers. Carried to its extreme, an adversarial relationship becomes hostile, and morale deteriorates. Not much work gets done, either.

Fortunately, Tennant Company has a history of good relationships between workers and managers. It has always been known as a well-run company and a good place to work. But as we became more deeply involved in the quality process, we began to see barriers to cooperation we hadn't realized existed. Some of those were barriers between levels; others were barriers between work groups and departments.

There were barriers caused by blame. In manufacturing and assembly, the introduction of the ECI (Error Cause Identification) forms spurred considerable discussion about who was to blame for defective parts or production mistakes. The blame always fell to the other person or department. The same kind of finger pointing also took place between divisions: sales people blamed shipping when machines were delivered damaged or late; shipping blamed order processing; order processing blamed manufacturing, and so on.

There were barriers caused by distrust. Even when managers believed that zero-defects programs would improve the quality of work life at Tennant Company, employees had to be convinced. They didn't really trust management's motives in establishing zero-defects programs. They suspected the quality emphasis was a management "fad," a gimmick to make employees work harder, or to quit if they failed to meet standards. Many employees believed quality was a temporary campaign that would fade when executives turned their attention to other matters. In other words, employees didn't trust management, and there were problems of trust and blame throughout the company that were barriers to cooperation. To reduce those barriers, we began to look at all aspects of management/worker relationships in our company.

First, managers and supervisors increased the amount of time they spent among employees. They asked questions. They listened. They made themselves available. They let it be known they were there to help with problems, not find fault. Supervisors moved their desks out from behind glass doors onto the manufacturing floor. The doors of the managers' offices were opened. Companywide, we made an effort to eliminate the red tape that hindered communication and cooperation.

As a result, we have seen marked improvement in the relationships between managers and supervisors and the employees who work with them. Supervisors trust employees to do quality work, and employees trust that if there is a problem, the supervisor will do something about it. That trust is built on experience, and the experience is the result of our company-wide effort for quality.

The improved management/employee relationships are explained by one employee. "When people are responsible for good quality, they feel proud of what they're doing. They work together and are receptive to change. Tell them specifically what you want, make them accountable, and support them by providing the resources they need. They are going to feel good, and as a result, our quality will be high."

Cooperation occurs when everyone is working toward a common goal.

The quality process also improved relationships among departments. For example, the engineers responsible for new product design had chronic difficulty with the production groups they called on to develop new machines, so they organized a small group with representatives from those production groups to look at communication problems. They found that most people in the company had no idea what was involved in new product development. Now, charts outlining the process of creating new products can be seen in meeting rooms around the company. For each new product, a team is formed with members from the various areas that will be involved.

Another serious barrier was discovered between engineering and manufacturing when Tennant Company began its ECI program. The people on the floor had to be convinced that engineers would pay attention to their problems. As one member of the welding department recalls, "Before, to get an engineer to come down to look at a problem was a real hassle. They didn't have time, they had things to do that were more important." When a problem arose for a welder, it could stop work until a solution was found. The engineers rarely shared that sense of immediacy. "Now," the welder says, "when you need an engineer, all you have to do is get on the phone, and they'll break a leg to get down here." The engineers proved themselves by responding to ECI forms. Now the forms are often bypassed, and, as the welder says, a phone call brings instant attention.

In addition, the ad-hoc groups formed to work on specific problems helped alleviate the adversarial relationships among departments. When members of separate work groups come together to solve a common problem, they learn to appreciate their ability to help one another, and blame is replaced by cooperation. Says one welder: "Cooperation is better across the company. It used to be that when we had NSR (non-standard reports) charges for doing things wrong, one department would blame it on the next. Now, if there is a problem in assembly, they come and *talk* to us. They ask us what we think went wrong. A lot of respect has grown up between departments. We see that the machinists, the sheet metal fabricators, the tool and die makers are all working on their own quality. That makes our job a lot easier."

Finally, where quality is concerned, we believe the management team has earned the trust of the other people in the company. There is no question that quality is "first among equals," and it is here to stay.

Something in It for the People

In the people themselves lie the knowledge and the energy to translate attention to quality into measurable results.

For a quality effort to have lasting impact, there must be something in it for the people, some incentive to participate and make individual commitments to its success. That "something" can take three forms—recognition, reward, and satisfaction.

Recognition can be powerful. We see its effect at the annual recognition dinners when award recipients receive their plaques or rings. We see it in a collection of "That-A-Way" notes tacked to an office worker's wall. We see it when a supervisor says, "You're doing a great job," and slips a small box containing a Tennant Company quality gift onto a desk or work station. Recognition makes people feel good.

But recognition is not the only way to reward. The Tennant Company suggestion program, in which employees who recommend changes are awarded 20 percent of the company's first-year savings directly related to those recommendations, also builds enthusiasm for individual and group contributions to the quality process.

The Tennant Company suggestion program has been in place since the mid-1940s. When we realized it could be a powerful tool for quality, we renamed and formalized it. Recognizing that improvements can save money, we created guidelines and a form that both individuals and groups can use when submitting their ideas. Now called S.W.A.T. (Stop Waste At Tennant), the program has saved the company thousands of dollars and returned a proportionate amount to those individuals and groups (called S.W.A.T. Teams) making suggestions (see appendix for suggestion form).

The opportunity to make work more satisfying is probably the strongest and most lasting reason for a sustained interest in quality. Employees are satisfied with their jobs and in their work when they know they can make a difference. At Tennant Company, the story of the company's welders best illustrates what can happen when employees make this discovery.

When the Welding Department received its first Group Quality Recognition Award in 1983, only newcomers to the company would have been unaware of the award's significance. Five years earlier, this department of 37 had been the company rebels. They were rough, burly young men whose Harley-Davidson motorcycles, lined up outside the factory, symbolized their self-image. They wore drab army-surplus fatigues as protection from the flying sparks, and that unofficial uniform set them apart from other production workers. The welders worked by their own rules and set their own standards.

In 1981, the night-shift welders were assigned a new supervisor who took a fresh look at the department's work patterns. He saw a number of procedures that hampered productivity. The group began to work on ways to increase productivity. The supervisor made a chart that showed the department's improved productivity. Before long, members of the night welding shift were turning in suggestions for improving efficiency. These were submitted to the company's cash-award suggestions program. The welders made their suggestions as a group, not as individuals. Their ideas led to increased profits for the company, and they used the cash returns for group camping and boating trips. Slowly, these rugged individualists coalesced into a team.

The opportunity to make work more satisfying is probably the strongest and most lasting reason for sustained interest in quality.

During the next year, some members of the night-shift crew and their supervisor transferred to the day-shift section. There, the supervisor became interested in a productivity effort called RISLIP (Reduce Inventory, Space, Labor; Improve Productivity), and began to talk with his section workers about how it might be achieved. Traditionally, the welding department's procedure was to weld several individual machine parts—frame sides or brush wraps, for example—then send them to the stockroom, where they were stored until the department had an order to produce a particular machine. The company's engineers wanted to streamline the operation by welding more and storing fewer units. They devised a system with a $100,000 price tag that was rejected by management as too expensive. Even a scaled-down, $25,000 version was deemed too costly.

A small group of welders tackled the problem. They designed an overhead monorail that could carry welded parts from one station to another so a frame could be welded together from start to finish without leaving the department.

The welders weren't deterred by cost. They discovered a supply of I-beams in a local junkyard and bought them for less than $2,000. In two days they installed the monorail. In the first year of its use, the new system saved Tennant Company more than $29,000 in time and storage space.

In the meantime, the welding supervisor was carefully documenting the cost of quality in his department. In 1981, he calculated, the welding department's annual cost of quality was $73,186. A whopping 2,939 hours were spent on rework—correcting procedures *not* done right the first time. Within two years, the welders reduced their cost of quality to $11,794 and cut rework hours to 249.

Those dramatic reductions were achieved by small groups tackling specific problems—inefficient set ups, for instance. In 1982, the welders were setting up their jobs at 54.7 percent of industrial engineering standards for efficiency. A group of five welders, one from each section, met to work out a system for improving that percentage. They made scheduling changes, grouping several small jobs together on pallets so they could all be done by the same welder. They assigned larger jobs to a single welder who could improve his own methods to save time overall. A year later, the welders' average set-up rate was 78 percent of the engineering standard. Those improvements led to the department's first Group Quality Recognition Award in late 1983.

But the welders didn't stop there. By mid-1984, welding's set-up efficiency had increased to 90 percent, saving $45,000 a year for Tennant Company. A productivity improvement team began converting welding's inventory ordering for major components to a "Just-in-Time" system that would save Tennant Company $100,000 every year.

What's in it for the welders? Satisfaction. In the words of one: "I feel like I am part owner of this company. I know that if I have a complaint about anything, it will be heard—not always answered to my satisfaction, but heard. I am going to do anything I can to make this company a success and the quality process a success. I'm happy being a welder, but when I have an opportunity to be part of a group working in another area, I jump at the chance. I really want to share what I've learned. The more people know about the quality program, about productivity, about the company, the more they are going to support what we're doing."

As one Award of Excellence recipient notes, "If you recognize people for their jobs, they're going to try harder and feel better about themselves."

Time, Energy, and Determination

Quality is a marathon, not a sprint.

Like any other worthwhile effort—whether it is training for a long-distance race, preserving a good marriage, or successfully shedding excess pounds—quality takes time, energy, and determination. The quality effort must be made so integral to everyday operations and the thinking of employees at all levels that it becomes part of every activity. It must become part of a company's woodwork. And that means nothing less than a change in a company's culture—the values and attitudes that underlie its relationships with customers, employees, and suppliers.

Japanese products are the best example of what can be achieved with time, energy, and determination. Forty years ago, they were synonymous with "cheap." The Japanese set out to change that image. They knew it wouldn't happen overnight—or even in a few years. But happen it did. The Japanese had patience and determination, even though 25 to 30 years passed before they were recognized as manufacturers of quality products.

At Tennant Company, we also have taken the long view. To do so runs counter to the prevailing attitudes of many American businesses, where short-term profit takes precedence over long-term investment. We know that a permanent change in our culture will be achieved because we already have evidence that it is happening.

We recognize that change takes more than just time. We keep reminding ourselves that it also takes energy, both from the company and from individuals.

It takes energy to solve problems in groups. Every group has its own life and process, and the individuals in it must expend energy both on learning to work together and on the problem they're hoping to solve.

It takes energy to put another Quality Team in place, and energy from the members of the team to set goals and then achieve them. Every ZD Day takes energy; so does every joint meeting with the Japan Management Association, where our focus is on quality.

The fact that we are willing to expend that energy, for as long as it takes, is testimony to our determination. At Tennant Company, we are determined to build quality into every product we make and into our work every day.

Drilling for Quality

To some people, drilling precision holes in machine parts may sound tedious. What challenge could there possibly be for quality, or what need for zero defects in holes drilled?

But Ed Mingo, former machinist, says the job can be a quality challenge. "The challenge comes in setting up the machine for new parts. If it is set up incorrectly, the parts will be defective."

Ed's goal was to produce defect-free parts. He also set—and met—efficiency, safety, and absenteeism goals. But he didn't stop there. In 1983, he began meeting once a month with a tool crib attendant and supervisor to find ways of increasing efficiency in getting tools and equipment from the tool crib. Their goal was to reduce the time the machine operators spent going to the tool crib and waiting while the right tools were pulled for their next job.

Ed and the tool crib attendant devised a "pull sheet" on which the tools needed for each job are listed (the specific drill fixture, drills, and gauges, for example). With that sheet, the attendant can pull the proper tools beforehand and deliver them to the operator's work station when-needed. The operator can complete one job and immediately set up his machine for the next one. This process eliminates the time the operator spent going to the tool crib, waiting while the attendant pulled the tools, and returning to the work station.

Says Ed: "Quality is a team effort, and everything has to mesh together. If you do your job right, it makes it easier for everyone else to do their jobs right." **R.K.**

THREE

TOOLS FOR THE MANAGER

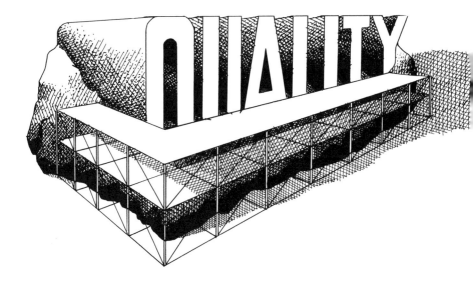

TOOLS FOR THE MANAGER

Management support and enthusiasm are the keys to starting and maintaining a quality emphasis. If a company's managers care, employees will care. But change is hard. If managers are to support a program of change, they must stand to gain from that program.

Tennant Company's quality process has made management jobs more secure and personally enriching, and it has provided opportunities for financial reward. Managers know this now, but in the beginning no one knew how the quality process would affect his or her job. And no one knew if it was here to stay or even if the company's CEO was solidly behind the effort.

So the first step in marshalling management support is to communicate top management's long-term commitment to the quality process. As we mentioned earlier, we launched a number of activities aimed at doing just that. These included staging the first ZD Day, publicizing throughout the company the quality pledges signed by our executives, and forming a Quality Team made up of representatives from all departments.

The next step is to explain to managers and supervisors what the process entails and to define their roles in that process. At Tennant Company, members of our first Quality Team led managers and supervisors through a review of Phil Crosby's 14 steps to quality, and outlined five ways in which the process must be supported:

- **Knowledge**—Managers and supervisors must know enough about the program to explain it to their employees.
- **Attitude**—They must be positive about the program.
- **Example**—They should set an example of doing the job right the first time.
- **Training**—They must make sure their employees know what is expected of them and have the skills or training needed to do the job.
- **Recognition**—They should acknowledge employees for jobs well done.

In explaining Crosby's 14 steps to quality, we were also offering managers and supervisors a reason to buy into the process—job security. Because we had a history of profit sharing, good benefits, and promoting from within, our people already understood the connection between their job security and the health of Tennant Company. With Crosby's 14 steps they now had a way to contribute to the company and their own well-being.

We also provided managers the opportunity to directly benefit from supporting the quality emphasis by changing their compensation program. Traditionally, part of the compensation package for salaried employees was based on achieving certain annual goals. We now asked our salaried people to make one of those goals quality related.

Ultimately, there was another, more intangible advantage for managers and supervisors who supported the quality process, but it was one they had to learn from experience. Specifically, the process can and has made some jobs easier and the working environment more pleasant.

As one supervisor said, "Quality is not just the quality in a piece of equipment; it is the quality of how you treat each other. Now we go after the reasons why something went wrong, not after people. Just eliminating finger pointing makes my job easier. And I feel more secure and confident knowing that no one is going to point a finger at me.

"I depend on my people to produce good quality parts. And they depend on me to find a solution if there is a problem that prevents them from doing their jobs right."

This kind of interdependence can drastically reduce the pressure managers personally feel to cross every "t" and dot every "i." But interdependence is only possible when managers and supervisors transfer some of their power to their people, so those people can truly become responsible for the work they do.

Occasionally a transfer of responsibility results in the elimination of some management jobs. When employees do their jobs right the first time, the need for people in inspection and rework is dramatically cut. In addition, employees need less supervision as they take greater control over their jobs and their output.

At Tennant Company, some jobs were eliminated because of changes brought about by the quality process. Many of these changes were absorbed through attrition and retirement. Rather than rehire, we moved people around. Other changes were addressed by re-training and career counseling.

Offering re-training and career counseling not only looks at the issue of job elimination, it also opens opportunities within the company and reduces job burnout. And this helps us keep good people who want to change jobs but don't want to change companies.

The quality process challenges a company to create an interdependent and responsible work environment. The responsibility for doing this lies with the manager, and to operate effectively, managers need the tools outlined here: communication, training, error-cause identification, small groups, goal setting, and recognition.

Communication
Communication is knowing how to elicit clear, concise feedback from people, knowing how to set goals and communicate them to employees, and knowing how to acknowledge the accomplishments and efforts employees make every day.

If we'd been asked to name some of our major problems when we began our quality process, communication would not have been mentioned. We thought communication within Tennant Company was excellent.

Once a month, a general meeting involving every employee was held in each department. We would talk about what was happening in the company, in the department, in other departments, and how we were doing financially. We knew of few other companies that communicated in this way.

In addition, we had the traditional communication vehicle, the company newsletter, to keep us informed of corporate news, policy changes, promotions, anniversaries, and birthdays. On a more informal basis, managers in one department kept in touch with their personnel by spending time each week in the production area.

There is nothing inherently wrong with these communication activities, which are still an ongoing part of the culture at Tennant Company. But they do not comprise a communications process, and engaging in them did not automatically mean we were good communicators, as we had mistakenly assumed.

Communication, our first Quality Team told us, involves knowing how to elicit clear, concise feedback from people, knowing how to set goals and communicate them to employees, and knowing how to acknowledge the accomplishments and efforts employees make every day. In all of these areas, the team said, Tennant Company managers were not communicating.

Managerial skills can rise to the level demanded by the quality process only with these communication skills. And these skills can be acquired only with the most basic communication skill of all—listening.

Although listening is the most fundamental communication skill, it is also the one most often taken for granted. Listening is hard work. It requires us not only to hear, but also to interpret and evaluate. Only then can we really respond and complete the communication cycle. When the cycle is complete, we have a common ground for understanding.

There are many resources available for learning how to listen. Tennant Company turned to the company whose name was practically synonymous with listening, Sperry Corporation (now Unisys). Sperry provided us with materials it had been using in its listening courses, and referred us to its consultant, Lyman Steil. A former professor at the University of Minnesota, Steil currently heads his own consulting firm, Communication Development Inc.

Two of our trainers attended Steil's course on listening. They and another employee then designed an in-house course, using information from Steil, Sperry, and several other sources.

The first people to attend the five-part course were executives and managers from manufacturing. Eventually, every manager and supervisor in the company attended, either voluntarily or at the request of their bosses.

Some of these graduates then asked the trainers to present a condensed version of the course to their line people during the time set aside for departmental meetings. In the past five years, about one-third of all our employees have had either full or partial training in how to listen.

The full course involves four sessions, each two-and-one-half hours long and covering a specific topic or exercise as follows:
- why we need to listen
- how to listen actively by paraphrasing the message and relaying it back to the sender
- resolving conflict with good listening techniques
- role playing
- video taping role playing for later critique

The second part of our communication program, called "Working Together," is about how we express ourselves to one another. This five-part course covers the following topics:
- understanding yourself
- understanding others
- developing styles of communication
- mapping issues (which includes identifying issues, contracting to work together, identifying intentions and generating solutions)
- building self-esteem

As with the listening course, we went outside the company to set up the program. Our primary consultant was Sherod Miller, president of Denver-based Interpersonal Communications Programs Inc. and one of the authors of the workbook, *Working Together.*

All our managers and supervisors received in-house verbal communications training. Some line people also received the training at the request of their department managers.

The listening and verbal skills courses helped us realize what our individual responsibility is in the communication process. We know listening is important; it takes energy, and personal bias can get in the way of how accurately we receive a message. We know it is our responsibility to ask for more information when we need it and to ask for clarification if a message seems vague.

The courses had another very important effect: they fostered employee involvement in small groups and in the quality process because they convinced people their input could make a difference and they could be heard.

In a company our size it takes about two years to train all the managers and supervisors. It is therefore important to make the programs available continuously. So far, we have not found it necessary to offer refresher courses in listening and verbal communication. But some of the principles we learned from these courses have been built into other training programs in group process skills and performance appraisals.

Training for the Long Haul

Training takes time.

Training is an integral part of the quality process, and as ongoing as the process itself. Basic problem solving requires training; advanced problem solving requires training. Preventing problems requires training.

Tennant Company's training program provides people with the tools they need to do the job right the first time. Our traditional approach to training, which was confined to on-the-job instruction and selected management seminars, could not answer the demands of the quality process.

The quality process requires that employees know how to communicate, how to set goals, how to measure progress, how to solve problems, and how to work together in groups.

These five "how-to" categories form the backbone of our training program, and are discussed individually in other sections of this book. Other courses, such as value analysis and time management, for example, fill out the training schedule. (See appendix for a listing of courses.)

We had no long-range training program outlined when we began the quality process. We did not have

If you think training is expensive, consider the price of ignorance.

a full-time trainer. For the most part, the program evolved as the process challenged us to master new skills and as our people became better able to identify their own training needs. When we started, we knew that managers and supervisors, who were expected to carry the process forward, would need to be schooled in the fundamentals. By the end of 1983, they had taken classes in developing quality measurements, setting quality goals, applying costs to quality measurements, and recognizing and supporting the achievements of employees.

Managers and supervisors, in turn, began giving us feedback on what training would be useful for their people. Many of them, for example, requested communications training and made time available for it during departmental meetings.

Based on that feedback, which we solicited through a needs assessment survey, we were encouraged to continue our basic courses in communications and problem solving. Some of the most frequent requests were for courses in decision making, performance appraisal, interviewing, and career development.

Everyone at Tennant Company is eligible for some type of training on company time. We ask that employees elect job-specific courses and that they discuss training needs with their supervisors beforehand. Another avenue to training sessions may be when supervisors request that some courses be mandatory.

To make sure employees are aware of available training courses, we print and distribute training calendars. The calendars, updated every six months, list when and where the courses are held, whether they are companywide or department-specific, and who can attend.

Our program runs the gamut from ongoing courses in subjects such as time management, to one-time courses in response to specific management needs, to technical courses such as torque training or blueprint reading.

The courses are taught by our human resource trainer, our technical trainer, or, occasionally, by employees. Most of the courses we teach have been designed by our trainers, sometimes with the help of an outside consultant, and draw on material from several sources.

When we began our quality process in 1979, we found that 85 percent of the total cost of quality was failure cost associated with not doing things right the first time. Another 12 to 13 percent was spent in appraisal or inspection. Only 2 to 3 percent went to prevention, which primarily involved training. Because of our quality emphasis, those ratios have changed: By 1986, 42 percent of the cost of quality was attributed to rework, 17 percent to inspection and 41 percent to prevention.

Training takes time. Our supervisors and managers have all been through at least five training courses. About 90 percent of our line workers have been involved in at least one training program.

With a work force of 1,300, training hours add up. In 1984, our trainers conducted 300 hours of classes. The same was true in 1985. In both those years, about 700 employees signed up for classes.

Though we cannot attach bottom-line figures to the benefits of training at Tennant Company, we do know it has paid off in reduced errors on the job. And we also know the truth of the slogan that is prominently displayed in Ron's and Doug's offices: "If you think training is expensive, consider the price of ignorance."

Pinpointing Problems and Identifying Causes

Employees need to be involved not only in detecting problems but in solving them.

Unlike nearly every other aspect of the quality process at Tennant Company, our Error Cause Identification (ECI) program is becoming obsolete. That makes us happy because it means two things: We have drastically reduced our errors, and we have dramatically improved our ability to communicate directly with each other.

We use the ECI program to pinpoint problems that prevent people from doing their jobs right the first time. The process begins when employees fill out a form listing snags that prevent them from doing their assigned jobs. Without this information, the quality process can't proceed.

Trying to solve the problems employees listed led us to form small groups. The problems were too numerous and varied for just a few people to handle. Because we asked employees to get involved, not only in detecting problems, but in solving them, our people began to understand that they really could make a difference in how Tennant Company operated.

NUMBER OF ECIs SUBMITTED

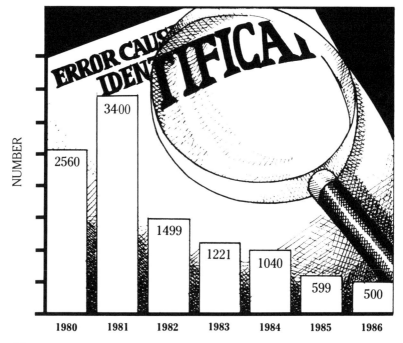

At first we made the ECI forms available only to employees at one facility. Based on the enthusiastic reception there, we introduced them to the manufacturing department and then to the rest of the company.

Those early forms were complicated, with elaborate codes and questions. But employees seized the opportunity to explain obstacles they encountered on the job, noting everything from inadequate equipment to unclear or mismatched blueprints.

The first year we took the ECI program companywide, the forms hit us with the speed and force of a mountain snowstorm. Our evaluators, those employees designated to resolve the problems, were buried under 3,400 forms. The evaluators painstakingly reviewed them, making sure the right people became involved in seeking solutions.

Because there were too few evaluators reviewing too many forms, which were often hard to decipher, we feared the ECI program would create more problems than it would solve. Employees became increasingly frustrated as weeks, and sometimes months, went by before anyone acknowledged or addressed their problems.

To eliminate the backlog, we increased the number of evaluators and simplified the form. We asked evaluators to meet one-on-one with the people who had initiated the forms so they could more precisely understand the problem. If the initiators were satisfied that the evaluators understood the problems, they signed the form and the evaluators went to work on solutions. If initiators were not satisfied, they could ask their managers or supervisors to intervene.

One-on-one talks between initiators and coordinators produced two results: 1) initiators knew that their problems had been acknowledged and understood, and 2) evaluators had more time to spend solving problems rather than sending the ECI forms back to the initiators for clarification.

We are now completing 90 percent of all ECIs within 30 days. ECIs that are unsolved after 60 days go to a management committee for review.

ECI forms are available in our plants and offices throughout the country. They are sent to three coordinators in Minneapolis who keep track of the paperwork and follow up on forms that evaluators find hard to handle.

Early in the program, the coordinators, who have other job responsibilities, spent nearly all their time with the ECIs. Now they each spend about four hours a week on ECIs.

Overall, the number of ECIs has dropped from a peak of 3,400 in 1981 to about 500 in 1986. This doesn't mean we only have 500 problems in the company. It does mean we're learning how to work together to solve the problems we do have without filling out forms. We hope to eliminate the ECI system within the next few years as people develop trust in the informal system.

Super Saturday

"Super Saturday" is now part of Tennant Company's folklore. It occurred the first year we issued ECI forms, when our engineers were falling behind in their efforts to correct problems pinpointed in ECIs.

On Saturday, January 10, 1981, 65 engineers, managers, and support people came in to work on the backlog of problems that needed corrective action. Most were requests originating in manufacturing, and on Super Saturday, 70 were pulled from the stack and assigned to engineering staff members. They were a blur of activity as they scurried about, looking up bills of material on computer terminals, calling up prints from microfilm files, and consulting with co-workers on where to find the information they needed to solve particular problems.

The problems they tackled that day were as varied as the methods for investigating and solving them. One engineer was asked to determine why a certain model TENNANT machine always had an extra grommet. Another investigated the possibility of eliminating an unneeded hinge on another model. A third tried to find out why a hose on a particular model tended to become caught between the tank and a tire.

Not all of the 70 problems were completely solved that day. But Super Saturday participants learned a valuable lesson—how difficult it is to make a product when specifications are wrong, incomplete, or difficult to understand. Said one engineer: "We learned first-hand how important it is to do it right the first time." **D.H.**

The Fastener Committees

Tennant Company customers include some of the largest manufacturing companies in the country, among them the car makers. In 1978, the following incident with one of the biggest car makers began a long quest for quality led by Daryl Gabrielson, designer of floor scrubbers.

The auto maker had just purchased the largest scrubber Tennant Company makes. But all was not well. Daryl's boss came to him with a request: "How would you like to go to Detroit? The customer has some questions about the design of our squeegee linkage. Maybe you could help."

Daryl wasn't alarmed. He had just redesigned the squeegee, and it probably needed adjusting to the customer's floor.

But he quickly found that more than a minor adjustment was needed in Detroit. He was greeted in the auto maker's maintenance department: "If you don't put this thing together right now, you can take it back to Minneapolis."

When the scrubber was delivered to the customer's dock, bolts and nuts were loose everywhere. What was worse, this wasn't the first time. Daryl had heard complaints from service trainers who helped local service and salespeople uncrate and install new machines. They were often told to bring their tool kits to put the machine together before it could be used.

Long before his trip to Detroit, Daryl had been trying to develop a standard for fasteners. The design groups for each of Tennant Company's three major products wanted different sizes, types, makes, and quality of nuts and bolts. Although the situation was an organizational nightmare, even the design chief and the keeper of our standards weren't convinced of the need for consistency. However, the Detroit problem was impossible to ignore.

We wish we could say that once the problem was recognized, it was solved immediately. But even in a company paying great attention to quality, problems sometimes are not easily solved. In fact, it took eight years. Without Daryl, we might still have problems keeping our machines together.

After his Detroit report, Fastener Committee #1 was organized.

Four months later, in March 1979, Fastener Committee #2 was formed. All of its members were new—except for Daryl. They looked at the clamping issue left over from committee #1 and checked into buying some new tools. After much research, they recommended switching from grade 2 to grade 5 hardware. It was a drastic step, fraught with implications: Where was all the grade 2 hardware? How would we collect it? How would we convince the assemblers it wasn't the right quality for our application? After all, they'd been using grade 2 for years.

To our surprise, the assemblers were ready for a change. They'd been frustrated by fastener heads breaking off and were tired of drilling out bolts.

At the same time, our tool supplier recommended we use torque tool equipment. Breaking off the heads of bolts was a sign of over tightening. The torque tool would shut off when the correct tightness was achieved. The assemblers wouldn't have to guess when to shut off the pneumatic air tools, the supplier said.

Well, the assemblers didn't appreciate the suggestion that they were guessing. Some of them had been assembling machines for 10 years. The torque equipment recommendation was tabled, and Fastener Committee #2 continued investigating what it would take to upgrade fastener hardware.

In January 1980, Fastener Committee #3 got under way. Once again, all the members were new—except for Daryl. This committee decided to concentrate on a one-time hardware changeover. But it found that you can't just change from one grade to another without affecting other types of hardware. It recommended hardened flat washers, grade 5 nuts, flat socket head screws and elimination of spring lock washers.

Two years later, in April 1982, Fastener Committee #4 was organized. All the members were new—except Daryl. The supplier had given the company a quote of $92,000 to change to torque control tools. The company wasn't ready for that, but it was ready to implement the recommendations of committees #2 and #3. Tennant Company assemblers switched to grade 5 hardware, obtained hardened flat washers, and eliminated spring lock washers.

The committee was on a roll. It reviewed current product models for improper hardware. It changed and updated methods and put together a pictorial instruction book for all 75 assemblers to show how to put the machines together.

By this time, Daryl had an ally. Dave Sorenson, an industrial engineer, had joined him in his fight for standardized fasteners. Dave had served on committee #4, and he was in too far to get out.

Daryl and Dave set up control charts to monitor (with the newly purchased testing equipment) the reliability of the tools being used by the assembly line. They completed a Fastener Standards Book. Hardware was reduced from 1,200 varieties to 900. From now on, design teams had to have approval from Daryl before ordering any new hardware. He was also to be included on new product team meetings to discuss questions about clamping bolts to joints and to make recommendations about other hardware.

In November 1983, the last committee—Fastener Committee #5— was formed. Members included the vice president of engineering and manufacturing, the new test equipment auditor, the final inspection supervisor, the company's technical trainer—and Daryl and Dave. For the next three years, team members worked together like a finely tuned orchestra. They set their goal: no loose fasteners by December 1985. With the support of the vice president on the team, they recommended purchase of the new torque control equipment—even though the cost estimate had gone from $92,000 to more than $200,000. The trainer put in place a three-part course required of every employee who had anything to do with fasteners. Between January and August 1984, 230 manufacturing and engineering employees were trained. Each one received a torque control book—the basic manual.

In January 1985, the 230 employees who had received torque training were given a one-hour update session. Still, committee #5 was not sure that everyone was using the new tools. It knew many of the old-style pneumatic tools were tucked away, and some were being used. One afternoon just before quitting time, the committee members rolled carts onto the assembly floor and collected the last of the pneumatic guns. They found them hidden in shoes and desks, fastened under work benches with magnets, hidden under rags. Some of their owners yelled and cursed. Others said the team members wouldn't be able to sleep nights because of what they'd done. Still, the committee was determined. By the end of the year, the group achieved its goal. The torque equipment worked, and there were no loose fasteners.

By 1986, the last committee could turn over its work to assembly supervisors and employees. From that long experience we learned that any improvement in quality takes time, and that an overall commitment to quality achieves results. Without the quality emphasis, the teamwork and small group training, the torque program would never have survived.

Throughout this six-year journey, Daryl, Dave, and the technical trainer, Karen Glas, have become torque experts in the industry. If you ask Daryl how to get rid of loose fasteners, he'll reply, "You start with a trip to Detroit."

Small Groups Solving Problems

The primary medium for solving problems at Tennant Company is the small group.

The dominant pronoun at Tennant Company is "we." Small groups account for some of our most significant quality gains, such as the elimination of hydraulic leaks and the increase in shipments made on the day orders are received.

Solving problems in small groups is the antithesis of finger pointing, either outward or inward. Instead of placing blame, group members learn to empathize with people in different departments and seek common ground for solutions.

Since 1980, at least one-third of our work force has participated in small groups. One major factor in their success is that many are vertically integrated. This means they include not only people who have first-hand knowledge of the problems, but also people who can remove the obstacles to a solution once it is found. These are the "champions" we talked about earlier in this book.

We didn't learn to include all levels of management in small groups from a book, and we didn't observe it in traditional Japanese quality circles. We found it out along the way. Group participation is going to dwindle if solutions are continually thwarted because members of the group can't cross departmental lines, approve budget expenditures, or clear the way with top management.

This doesn't mean we require every group to have such a member. For example, if one small group is working on a limited problem and the solution needs only a supervisor's rubber stamp, that's fine. But small groups know they can recruit someone to run interference if necessary.

Another important element that has made small groups and many other aspects of our quality process successful is training. Small group members need technical and interpersonal training.

The technical training we used for small group skills was adapted from the Japanese Union of Scientists and Engineers (JUSE) manuals (the "red book" and the "blue book"). Our basic study course provides group members with these seven tools:

- brainstorming
- cause and effect diagrams
- pareto diagrams
- histograms
- checksheets
- graphs
- management presentations

This study course is under the direction of our manager of quality and test reliability. It requires at least 10 hours to complete; group members take it on company time. To date, most of the course graduates are from manufacturing or engineering, but requests for training are beginning to come in from other departments.

Our advanced study course was also adopted from the JUSE manual and is also directed by our quality manager. It runs the same length of time as the basic course, and covers subjects such as:

- sampling
- data collection and arrangement
- control charts
- stratification
- scatter diagrams

As the subject matter indicates, requests for this course come most often from various engineering departments, but many of our welders have taken it as well.

Small-group members can also take a course in group process skills, taught by our human resource trainer. This course first became available in 1984 in response to a training needs assessment survey. People said they needed to understand group dynamics and how to work together as a team.

Tennant Company's two-day group process skills course incorporates many of the fundamentals of listening skills and verbal communication. During one of its most useful lessons, the course encourages members to express their feelings and air their gripes, even if they seem peripheral to the problem at hand. Once members have a chance to vent their feelings, they are better able and more willing to concentrate on solving specific problems.

The group skills course also teaches us to diagnose how the group gets off track and how to redirect its course by confronting the "blocking dynamic," which could be caused by poor communication, lack of cooperation, or not having the people needed to solve the problem.

We believe another factor in group success is flexibility. We do not insist that our groups follow traditional quality circle guidelines in which groups are always ongoing and the supervisor is always the team captain. In fact, we encourage groups to limit their work to a specific problem. "We do this," one manager explained, "because quality circles can go on forever, and people end up meeting just for the sake of meeting. We want people to work together to solve a specific problem, then disband once that's done. In addition, traditional quality circles usually have the same members year after year. So the group loses its pizzazz."

At Tennant Company, we rotate membership in ongoing groups, such as the Quality Team and the ZD Day Planning Committee. Membership rotation not only broadens employee participation in groups, but brings a fresh viewpoint to the previous group's activities. New members can build on those activities without becoming married to them; they can introduce change when necessary.

There is also a great deal of flexibility in how groups form at Tennant Company. For example, anyone from a line person to a manager may decide to form a group. Or the impetus can come from the quality department because it collects and analyzes data from all departments, and its managers have a panoramic view of the problems and the problem solvers.

The quality department also helps managers introduce the small group concept by providing training and attending some meetings. This is what happened at Tennant Trend, Inc., a subsidiary that makes small commercial floor-cleaning products.

Tennant Trend management recruited members for the subsidiary's first problem-solving small group and provided them with a directive: "Find out what our biggest problem is." The group pinpointed backorders as the problem to attack and made it a goal to reduce backorders from 44 percent of all orders to zero percent.

Approximately 18 months after the group's solutions were introduced, backorders dropped to 10 percent, the average shipment time of backorders decreased from 45 days to 30 days, and Tennant Trend had saved at least $20,000. The group responsible for this has disbanded, but Tennant Trend is forming another group to solve a new problem: how to negotiate with vendors to reduce costs.

Though we put as few constraints on groups as possible, we do have one hard rule that always applies: groups must include people who will be directly affected by the group's work. This is probably why we have so many interdepartmental groups at Tennant Company. For example, in the area of new product design, group members will include people from various engineering departments (design, test, industrial and quality engineering), people from marketing, production control, production, material handling, and purchasing.

Working in small groups helps us recognize how our actions affect other people. It also reduces problems down the line because we coordinate our activities up front. In essence, groups help us understand that we have customers inside, as well as outside, the company.

Many of our managers and supervisors, especially in manufacturing and engineering, took the lead in encouraging the formation of small groups. They let employees know that management was serious about the program and that their participation was important. As soon as word spread about the success some of these groups enjoyed, new groups began to form spontaneously.

But small groups aren't going to be successful automatically.

Management has a responsibility to support them by making sure every group gets the members it needs. (We don't draft people, but we do draft job types.) Management also makes sure the group gets the training it needs and has the time to meet (usually one hour a week on company time). Management must also broadly approve of, if not direct, the goal set by the group. And, as we mentioned before, management must be willing to be part of the group if the group requests it.

The optimum group size is eight to ten people. Groups must include people who will be directly affected by the group's work.

We have found that the optimum group size, especially for those groups that form to solve a specific problem, is eight to ten people. If groups are much larger, it is difficult for everyone to speak during the one-hour meeting.

Finally, an element as essential to group success as it is to individual success is recognition. Recognition can be given in a variety of ways. At Tennant Company, we recognize group achievements in the company newsletter; we offer cash awards to groups that come up with ways to save the company money; we present outstanding achievement awards to groups. We also invite groups to set up display booths at ZD Day. At ZD Day III, one-half of Tennant Company's 80 operational groups took us up on this offer. Based on the interest those displays produced among our employees, we've decided to do this again on our next ZD Day.

Small Groups vs. Japanese Quality Circles

During the late 1970s, Americans heard and read a great deal about Japanese quality, management styles, and quality circles. Some of what I read made sense to me; some didn't. To find out more, Phil Crosby and I decided to go to Japan in 1980. We planned to visit a number of Japanese companies and find out more about their management and quality practices.

Thanks to the Tennant Company/Fuji Heavy Industries joint venture and Phil Crosby's reputation, we had access to top-level executives and managers in several companies. We asked them all similar questions with respect to quality circles and their effectiveness. We learned there is no typical Japanese company, just as there is no typical American one. We found as much variety among Japanese firms as we would find here. We did learn that almost every company uses quality circles. They're an institution. But we also learned that quality circles weren't the answer to every problem. In fact, our findings can be summarized in a statement by the president of one company. "Approximately 80 percent of our innovations, savings, and improvements come out of 20 percent of our quality circles. The other quality circles just meet. If I were an American manager," he added, "I would do things differently from the way we do them in Japan."

This was just the advice we were looking for. We asked him to elaborate. Here, in summary, are his recommendations:
- Make small-group participation voluntary.
- Organize each small group to attack a specific problem. When the problem is solved, dissolve the group. When another problem arises, form another group.
- Find a way to reward people who participate in small groups for their efforts. Specifically, make that reward consistent with the values of the people in that group.

In setting up our small groups at Tennant Company, we followed his advice. Groups are organized to solve specific, individual problems. Participation is voluntary, and no one is pressured by management to belong. And when a solution is found that saves the company money, the group receives a percentage of the first year's savings. **D.H.**

Setting Goals and Measuring Progress

People work better when they can define what "win" means on the job.

Americans like to know who's winning. Whether the game is baseball, bowling, or tennis, whether we're watching or playing, we want to know the score. Our experience at Tennant Company with setting goals and taking measurements taught us that the same is true in the workplace.

People work better when they can define what "win" means on the job. To keep score, people need to have goals and the skills and tools that allow them to measure their progress. Faith is not enough in the quality business.

Like many companies, our experience with goal setting was limited. Traditionally we asked only our managerial people to set goals, but we never gave them any standard guidelines to follow. We routinely took measurements in our manufacturing department. In other areas, people measured things we thought were important but which, we learned when we began listening to employees, contributed little to our understanding of how to do the job better.

All that had to change. For the quality process to work, goal setting had to become a company-wide activity, not an infrequent exercise. And the people who led the activity, the managers and supervisors, had to do so with some consistent skill.

The best way to proceed is slowly, setting highly achievable goals at first and then gradually setting more difficult, complex goals later. In 1980, we asked our managers and supervisors to set a goal for their groups or departments. Most set vague goals like, "I want to do better." That was fine as a warm-up; at least everyone had a goal.

A year later, we asked the managers and supervisors how they performed. Most didn't know because their goals were vague, and they didn't know how to measure their progress. At that point, we began a training program for all managers and supervisors.

Our purpose was to train managers and supervisors to identify and track problems that interfered with doing the job right the first time. Our major quality measurements began to take shape from the information we gathered during that process. We also taught our people how to apply costs to the quality measurements they were developing.

Next, we had to put those measurements in the context of goals. The manager of employment and development devised an in-house course to teach managers and supervisors how to set goals, how to get employees to participate in setting goals, and how to make goals meaningful. For a goal to be meaningful, it must be measurable, realistic, and attainable. It also has to be visible, so everyone knows what is expected. Many managers, for example, began putting their department's monthly, quarterly, or annual goals in chart form and posting the charts where all employees could see them.

We began handing out literature about goal setting. One of the best was a pamphlet called "Guide to Successful Goal Setting," published by Management by Objective Inc. The 37 steps outlined in the pamphlet are brief and to the point. They cover everything from the nature of goals to the expected results.

After the training was completed and managers and supervisors began to feel more confident about setting and measuring goals, they began to enlarge their scope, moving from department and group goals to quality and productivity goals. This evolutionary process took about four years. By starting with small, limited, achievable goals, people gradually gained the confidence to set bigger, more challenging ones.

The managers and supervisors, in turn, asked their people to set individual or group goals, depending on the nature of each person's job. Though we did not give line people formal training in setting goals, managers and supervisors did assist them. Goal setting became a standard practice throughout the company, and the goals were as varied as the jobs of the people who set them.

For example, the goals set and achieved by a service representative helped him win an Award of Excellence. He set three annual goals:

- to have 90 percent billable hours
- to sell at least 60 replacement brushes
- to contribute toward the sale of at least three machines

Tennant Company expects service representatives to spend most of their time serving customers. This representative quantified that expectation into a goal he could measure and achieve. The other two goals reflect his own initiative.

For example, the representative says he had sold brushes before, but just had not kept track of how many. Sixty brushes seemed like a realistic goal. And by giving customers the best possible service, and passing leads to salespeople, he knew he could contribute to machine sales.

This example is important because the representative set his own goals. No one else could have set goals that better used the representative's skills to make the greatest contribution to Tennant Company. We have found this to be true time and again, whether the job belongs to a service representative, a clerk, or a line worker. When people work with a supervisor setting their own goals, they have a great incentive to achieve them because they're the ones who created them.

We've come a long way from the days when all we measured was the manufacturing department's output. Every department in the company now has goals and ways to measure progress. And there are as many types of goals as there are jobs in the company, from production to service to office procedures. Even seemingly minor tasks such as returning phone calls or responding to Telex messages can be measured and performance improved by setting goals.

Setting and tracking goals unites work groups with a sense of purpose and a course of action. Our Oakland Service/San Francisco Sales Group came up with seven major one-year goals, including increasing sales of various products, increasing service reps' billable hours, and decreasing the number of unsatisfactory machine demonstrations due to machine failures. By year's end, the Oakland/San Francisco group had hit two goals and exceeded two others.

Goals are road signs on the quality journey. At Tennant Company, we include goals in all our product designs. These goals tell the designers, and everyone else concerned, including the people who manufacture the product and the people who sell it, what they can expect in terms of completion dates, warranty expense, and defects detected in final test.

We've also been able to set goals and measure progress in traditionally hard-to-quantify areas such as marketing. For example, our international marketing department, which coordinates international sales activities, has set a goal of three-day turnaround for handling orders, quotes, and complaints.

That's not always easy to achieve when you're dealing with calls and correspondence worldwide. But by tracking their turnaround time, department members became aware of the steps necessary to meet schedules, such as keeping a sufficient amount of printed material on hand and referring field people to their own manuals or brochures for answers to their questions.

Goals and measurements are road signs on the quality journey.

Goals provide an opportunity to recognize our own achievements and those of our co-workers. Small groups or departments, for example, often hold informal celebrations when they reach the goals they set. Frequently they're written up in our company newsletter. This kind of recognition gives us confidence in our ability to do our jobs right.

Recognition:
Keeping Feedback in the Forefront

Awards establish an ideal and encourage specific behavior that conforms to that ideal; positive feedback motivates employees to do their best each day.

Recognition, as we've said, is one of the most powerful tools for involving employees in a quality emphasis. The recognition program that evolved at Tennant Company over the past six years has two key elements: formal awards and informal recognition. The latter is more a process than a program, and it now goes on every day at the company.

Awards and informal recognition complement one another. Awards establish an ideal and encourage specific behavior that conforms to the ideal; positive feedback motivates employees to do their best each day. It is a medium for recognizing a broad number of people without invoking the "win/lose" attitude that awards almost inevitably generate.

We learned these lessons during our quality journey. We didn't realize the value of positive feedback until we were three or four years into the quality process. Like most companies, we thought about recognition in terms of awards. So in the beginning we focused on designing an awards program to acknowledge people's contributions to the quality emphasis. At the same time, we informally researched the recognition programs of other companies, but found little to emulate because we wanted to tie our awards specifically to quality.

We did, however, observe one characteristic that we wanted to avoid: having a management group or an executive select the award recipients. We felt that this would make the awards seem biased to the employees.

Eventually, we established three rules.

One, our program would be peer driven. An employee could nominate anyone of equal or lesser rank, but not anyone he or she reported to directly.

Two, recipients would be selected by a committee of employees of various ranks and from various departments in the company.

Three, we would establish a set of criteria for selecting recipients and print these criteria on the nomination forms. We created these guidelines, almost inadvertently, by asking ourselves what type of behavior we wanted to encourage. We came up with five behaviors that became benchmarks for judging individual achievement nominations:

1. Continuous superior performance in doing work right the first time over a minimum of one year
2. A cooperative, positive approach to problem solving
3. Taking the initiative in corrective action to solve problems (identifying errors, determining the cause of errors, correcting errors, or preventing errors)

4. Setting quality goals and demonstrating high-level effort to attain goals

5. Communications and other actions that support the quality process

As small groups sprang up at Tennant Company, we also decided to include group awards in our program. A group can be as few as two people or as many as a department. There are three group award criteria:

1. Continuous superior performance in doing work right the first time

2. Taking the initiative in corrective action to solve problems

3. Setting quality goals and demonstrating high-level efforts to attain goals

The review process for both individual and group award nominees is similar. As the nominations are received, the awards committee sends out questionnaires to people who are in contact with the nominees. The questionnaires help assess the individual or group's performance based on the awards criteria.

From these assessments, the committee assigns a value of one to five points for each criterion, then multiplies that total by the weighted value of each criterion. For example, the first and second individual award criteria are equal in value and higher than the other three criteria.

The committee usually makes its selections based on the highest scores, but occasionally changes the rankings to achieve a balance. This is done to prevent awards from being concentrated in one department or one type of job.

Individual awards are given annually to no more than 2 percent of the work force. Of that 2 percent, about one-third receives the Award of Excellence, a 10-carat gold ring with diamond chips around a stylized "Q." The others receive Special Recognition awards, 10-carat gold pins shaped like the Tennant Company Quality emblem. In addition, all recipients are given plaques.

The Group Excellence Awards are presented twice a year to no more than six groups each time. Each group member receives a gold pin, and the whole group shares the plaque.

We selected jewelry and plaques as award items because they best fit our requirements of making the awards visible and valuable symbols of the quality emphasis.

Our executives present the awards at formal banquets, one for individuals and two for groups. Recipients may bring a guest. We also acknowledge winners by writing about them in the company newsletter, posting bulletin board announcements, and engraving their names on a wall plaque in the reception area. In total, we spend about $50,000 a year on our formal awards program.

Although it is well suited to recognizing outstanding performers, this program has its limitations. The awards program takes place only once or twice a year and its narrow scope underscores the significance of the awards. By design, it leaves out a broad percentage of the work force.

The Koala T. Bear Award was designed to broaden recognition to more employees. We adopted the namesake of the award, a small, stuffed koala bear, as the mascot of our quality emphasis. The bear also occasionally appears in a cartoon in the employee newsletter.

The award is given monthly to employees who consistently meet their job standards and display a positive attitude. In addition to these essential criteria, nominees are reviewed on the basis of their special efforts in one of three areas: output, quality, or efficiency.

Like the formal awards program, this one is peer driven, so employees cannot nominate an immediate supervisor. A committee of people from various ranks and various departments makes the final selections.

Unlike the formal awards program, the committee for the Koala T. Bear Award asks people who benefit from the nominees' work to evaluate the nominations, and the number of winners is unrestricted. As few as two employees, or as many as 20, may qualify for the award in any given month.

The award, a certificate and a stuffed koala bear wearing a Tennant Company Quality T-shirt, is presented at work by a member of the committee. (The presentation itself is heralded by a committee member who dresses up in a bear costume.)

Even Koala T. Bear did not solve one nagging question: how to recognize employees daily for their efforts. In a survey, Tennant Company executives were asked by the CEO to rate the company on the eight hallmarks of outstanding companies named by the authors of *In Search of Excellence*. They rated the company low in one of those categories— employee recognition.

In Search of Excellence advocates the use of positive reinforcement. Our executives felt we slipped in providing reinforcement, and a subsequent survey of 200 employees selected at random supported their view.

To correct this imbalance, we formed a Positive Feedback Committee in 1984 to make recognition a larger part of our corporate culture. As one committee member put it, "We want people to enjoy coming to work, to think that work is fun, as well as something to do. Positive feedback is related to making people feel good about their jobs and wanting to do a good job." In short, recognition is a powerful motivator.

The committee created a positive reinforcement awareness campaign. They provided managers and supervisors with notepads printed with the slogan "That-A-Way" so notes can be written to employees for a job well done. The campaign also included posters and buttons urging everyone to give positive reinforcement, not just to think about how often they get it.

The team produced videos in which employees role played the "do's and don'ts" of positive reinforcement. For example, reinforcement should not contain a mixed message: "You're producing more parts, but unfortunately you're making more errors." After that kind of message, people will remember only negative comments. Whether it's positive or negative, feedback should be sincere, appropriate, and timely.

Recognition can be directed to groups as well as individuals. Small, informal celebrations are a good way to let groups of people know they are performing well. One manager, for example, brings coffee and donuts when his people hit their production quotas for the quarter. Others may bring in pizza for lunch. Such gatherings are inexpensive enough to be funded from petty cash, but they have a powerful effect in giving a group a sense of accomplishment. Many people feel this is an effective way of having an informal celebration.

The committee's efforts to improve positive reinforcement began to have an effect. In 1985, a survey of the same 200 employees revealed that they believed Tennant Company was doing a better job of recognizing employee effort. This "positive feedback" encouraged the committee to stay together for another year and work on ways to keep the issue of feedback in the forefront.

Recently, to meet this objective, the committee wrote and distributed a positive feedback mission statement that contains five key objectives:

- to enjoy working together
- to look for positives
- to understand and appreciate each other
- to build each other's esteem
- to handle negative situations in a positive way

The team also planned a long-range campaign to make more videos and to distribute packets of positive reinforcement information to managers and supervisors. Now, rather than the team holding meetings on topics, managers and supervisors will conduct them in their own departments.

As one employee expains, "Positive reinforcement makes people want to try harder. If you recognize them for something they tried, whether it was successful or not, at least you're supporting them for having tried. If you recognize them for having made the effort, you're going to get more."

FOUR

ACHIEVING RESULTS

ACHIEVING RESULTS

How long does it take to make a measurable difference with a quality emphasis? We have stressed that quality is a long-term effort because it involves changing a company's culture and laying a base for continued profitability. But the process can also yield many exciting short-term results that help build interest and maintain enthusiasm.

One way to achieve early results is to examine and change those procedures that exist just because "we've always done them that way." At Tennant Company, this led us to the rework area, which, unchecked by management, had grown in the 1970s.

By 1980, rework had swallowed 15 percent of our assembly space and threatened to claim more. We had an 80-by-120-foot bay teeming with machines that were either assembled incorrectly or were incomplete when they rolled off the line—usually due to problems with purchased parts.

In fact, rework was such an institution that rework jobs were the senior positions in production. Rework mechanics were able to log the most overtime, often working Saturdays so that machines could be shipped.

Our solution to this situation was drastic, and it had dramatic results. At Phil Crosby's urging, we cut the number of rework mechanics in half. Where there were 20, there would now be 10. (By 1986, that number had dropped to two.) Those from the rework area were transferred to other jobs in manufacturing, assembly, and service.

In addition to reducing expenses, these cuts in rework demonstrated that we meant what we said about achieving quality through preventive measures. To reinforce the message that we were going to build machines for shipment, not for rework, we converted part of the holding bay into a storage area for parts.

Our move worked. From 1980 to 1981, manufacturing rework time dropped from approximately 34,000 to 24,000 hours. As the quality process snowballed, our preventive measures cut rework time even further. By 1985, only 7,200 hours were spent fixing machines incorrectly or incompletely assembled. Over a five-year period, salaries paid to rework employees dropped from $425,000 to $174,000. Had we *not* cut manufacturing rework time, we would have been paying $527,000 in rework salaries by 1985.

Another Tennant Company practice that proved to be traditional rather than logical was our acceptance of a 5 percent error rate in inventory accuracy for material requirements planning. Again, at Crosby's suggestion, we made a dramatic change: we asked for 100 percent accuracy instead of 95 percent.

Within six months, inventory accuracy was up to 97 percent, the highest level the current system would allow. This resulted in fewer shortages on the assembly line and helped us with our material requirements planning in manufacturing.

Pilot programs are another way to achieve fast results and focus attention on a quality process. They also serve to involve groups of supervisors and hourly employees. That's what happened when we got a small group of mechanics and engineers together to work on streamlining production of our Model 432 walk-behind automatic scrubber. As we mentioned earlier, that group rearranged the assembly line so the Model 432 could be built and crated all in the same area. Within a year, this group had saved Tennant Company $19,000 and reduced the number of defects per machine.

Awareness Makes a Difference

Many of the dramatic results we achieved in the first few years of the quality process were mainly a function of awareness. Employees became aware of exactly what it meant to do their jobs correctly because job requirements were defined and/or refined. And as one employee explains, "It all comes down to attitude. When we publicize something like quality, it focuses attention and makes people start to look at what's going on." At Tennant Company, this was especially true in manufacturing and engineering, where the most dramatic changes were made.

Tennant Company management became aware of obstacles that might prevent employees from performing to meet requirements. During those first few years, we tended to tackle obvious problems that we were confident of solving. But the deeper we went into the process, the more profound were the problems we uncovered—profound in the sense that their solutions sometimes required radical changes, such as building products to order rather than forecasting and stocking them, or shipping our products crateless.

We also began to find ways to integrate the quality process into administrative areas. For example, in 1984 we established a formal cycle for counting inventory at the field warehouses. We found an accuracy level of 50 percent, which has since improved to 94 percent. This has greatly increased our ability to have the right part at the right place at the right time.

This high level of accuracy has also allowed Field Inventory Control to handle a higher volume of part numbers and an increased order volume by shifting order sources from Minneapolis to the field.

The Quality Diet

Actually, the quality process is like dieting. Results are usually the easiest and most dramatic in the early stages. The closer a dieter gets to his or her ideal weight, the more difficult losing weight becomes. And unless there is a fundamental change in eating and lifestyle habits, those gains will be lost as quickly as they were won.

That is why following Phil Crosby's 14 steps has proved so important for Tennant Company. Those 14 steps have done more than point the way to short-term gains and provide a regimen for keeping them. They have also provided us with a framework for changing our attitude toward the jobs we do, for redefining quality as something built in, not tacked on, and for understanding each other and our customers better.

We are finding it takes three cycles of Crosby's 14 steps over about a six-year period to make quality a part of a company's culture. Even at that, cultural changes do not take place at a uniform rate across the company. For example, the quality process at Tennant Company has proceeded much more rapidly in manufacturing and engineering than it has in other departments.

The quality process is like dieting.

But after three cycles of the 14 steps, we have at least reached a stage where we're no longer asking ourselves whether we should continue. Instead, we're asking specific questions like "Who will head ZD Day planning?" and broad ones like "How can we make the 14 steps more meaningful to administrative and engineering personnel?"

We are also finding that with each new cycle, the questions rising from the 14 steps become ever more sophisticated. For example, we are now trying to figure out the best way to use statistical process control as a tool for further quality improvement, set-up reduction, and improved reliability.

What Quality Means for Tennant Company

We were drawn to the quality process because of our desire to reduce costs and increase sales to make us more profitable. In 1980, for every dollar we grossed, we spent 17 cents working quality into our products. By 1985, we were spending only about 7.8 cents of each dollar on quality. We have come a long way to achieving our goal of reducing the cost of quality to 2.5 cents per dollar by 1988.

In previous sections, we have cited many examples of cost savings, such as $89,000 realized by shipping machines crateless and $40,000 a year achieved by the "Just-in-Time" inventory conversion in the welding department. But it is difficult to calculate just how much our quality emphasis has saved Tennant Company overall. We do know that since 1979, cost-reduction projects, the individual and group employee suggestion program, redesigned products and cost-avoidance gains have saved Tennant Company approximately $5.6 million.

The savings from the employee suggestion program reflect the influence of our quality process. In 1984, when teams as well as individuals became eligible for monetary rewards for their cost-saving suggestions, estimated annual savings from the suggestion program jumped to $200,010, up from $75,000 the previous year. In 1985, savings jumped to $481,000.

COST OF QUALITY

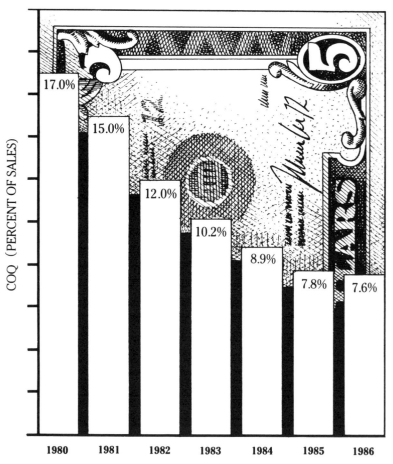

The team suggestion concept is clearly paying off. One group alone saved Tennant Company $64,150 annually by suggesting alternative methods of assembling our mid-size sweeper. The group that devised a work-cell concept saved us $75,000 in set-up time, material handling and inventory.

Most benefits of our quality process to date have been realized in the areas of manufacturing and purchasing, where the process began. Many of the savings the process netted have been applied to new product development, marketing, and new ventures.

Because we did not choose to convert all of these savings to the bottom line, we cannot attach an overall dollar amount to what the sav-

COST REDUCTION/SUGGESTIONS

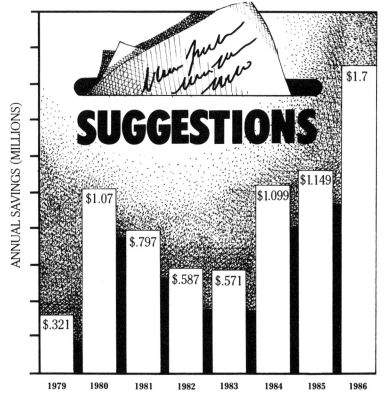

ings have meant to Tennant Company. But as the charts, graphs, and examples we've discussed indicate, the savings in many areas have been substantial and identifiable.

We believe the quality process is making an impact on our sales and profits. In the 1970s, our United States market share was about 60 percent. Today it is about 70 percent. The quality process is obviously having a positive effect on our reputation as a company.

What Quality Means to Customers

In 1985, we began a systematic survey of our customers. Each customer who purchased a TENNANT machine received a question-naire about a week after the machine arrived. The results of those ques-

PROBLEMS AT INSTALLATION

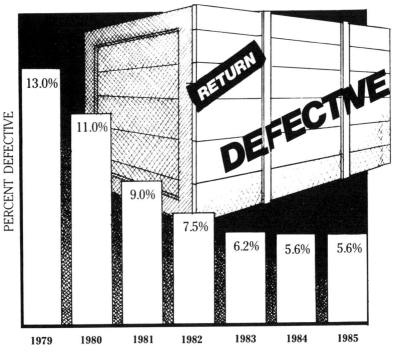

tionnaires assured us that our quest for quality was helping generate and maintain business. Our customers said that quality and machine performance were two of the three most important factors in their decision to purchase a TENNANT machine. (The third factor was the customer's previous association with TENNANT products.)

Ninety-five percent of those who returned our surveys said they were satisfied with our products, personnel, and support. We have no earlier surveys with which to compare these results, but we know that without the quality process we would not have scored as well.

For example, according to our installation reports, 13 percent of all machines shipped in 1979 had something wrong with them when they arrived at our customers' docks. Some of these defects were small,

SAME DAY PARTS ORDER PERFORMANCE

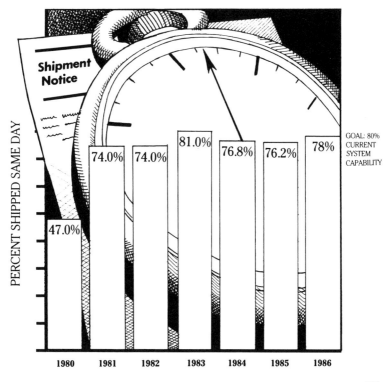

such as a damaged crate or a small scratch in the paint. Other defects were more severe, such as out-of-balance brushes on a sweeper.

By 1985, fewer than 6 percent of the machines shipped arrived with problems. And many of these problems, such as a missing manual, were not related to the machines themselves. Much of the credit for that reduction goes to the small group from the traffic, engineering, industrial engineering, and shipping areas that came up with plans for shipping some machines crateless, upgrading the quality of crates we did use, and developing a screening process for carriers much like the one we use to qualify suppliers.

Another measure of how the quality process has touched our customers is the same-day-order performance report. In 1980, fewer than half of supply- and repair-parts orders were shipped to customers the same day they were received. Now, 76 percent are shipped the same day. Our goal is to hit 80 percent; orders that arrive in late afternoon have to wait until morning.

The quality process has positively affected our service to customers in ways that are less easy to chart. For example, in 1982 we discovered an engineering flaw that caused some tanks on one model of scrubbers to leak cleaning solution. Subsequent tests revealed that if the tanks were going to leak, they would do so in the first or second year.

Traditionally, we would have waited for customers to call us if they ran into this problem. We then would have fixed it for free if the 12-month warranty were still in effect. If the warranty had expired, we charged the customer for fixing it. In other words, we just reacted to the problem.

Because of the quality process, we have become proactive rather than reactive. We alerted owners of this scrubber model to the potential problem and extended their warranties to three years. This cost us at least $1 million. We have no way to calculate the good will and credibility we gained with those customers, but we believe it was substantial.

Now, because we have eliminated so many flaws in design and assembly, we are able to offer customers a two-year warranty on new machines, the first in the industry. We also have a program called TED® (TENNANT Express Delivery). We promise the purchasers of new machines that we will deliver certain essential parts to them within 54 hours of receiving their orders. If we don't, the parts are free.

Even though we doubled the length of our warranty period and extended warranty coverage to more parts, our warranty expenses as a percentage of total sales remain well under one percent.

The gains we have made in customer service represent only a small fraction of what we intend to do. In fact, customer service is one of the key themes for Quality Team IV. The objectives of that team include:

- identifying internal and external customers
- identifying the needs of these customers
- evaluating current service levels
- improving processes and outputs to better meet customers' needs

One priority of Quality Team IV is to develop a customer assistance network. We believe we do a good job of responding to customer calls, but sometimes a customer will be bounced to three, four, or five people before connecting with the person who can really help.

We would like to funnel those calls through one person who is well versed in how the company works and how our machines work and who can direct the caller to the precise source of help. In addition, that person will log the calls and the nature of the problem, opportunity, or inquiry and follow up with solutions. In this way, we can begin to develop the equivalent of an ECI system for customers.

What Quality Means to Employees

A survey we conducted a few years ago showed that 66 percent of our employees believe the quality process has been of benefit to them. Though we did not ask employees to explain the benefits, we have observed some general improvements that have taken place in the workplace.

The first benefit has been the greater sense of control employees have over their jobs and the increased confidence they have in their ability to influence our environment. This stems from asking hard questions that lead to honest self-assessment, rather than to pointing fingers and passing the buck.

This assessment covers questions such as, Who will benefit from the job I do? Am I doing the job the right way? Do I have what I need to do the job? Is there help available for solving problems?

The training offered to Tennant Company employees goes a long way toward giving them problem-solving tools. These tools can be as concrete as pareto diagrams and flow charts or as abstract, but no less important, as the ability to communicate with others and work together in small groups.

It has taken time to achieve these results. According to a survey conducted in 1983, only a minority of our employees (31 percent in Minneapolis; 41 percent in the field) believed that we provided consistent support in helping them resolve problems. But in a 1985 survey, 56 percent of the employees said that their managers and supervisors frequently or always provided them with problem-solving support.

A second major benefit of the quality process is that it has enhanced self-motivation and given us a greater sense of purpose about the work we do. The 1985 survey results indicate that 86 percent of our people have their own job-related quality goals, set either by themselves or in conjunction with a supervisor. And 94 percent of them believe they have an effect on the achievement of departmental quality goals.

Right now, Quality Team IV is devising ways to answer questions that we have not yet addressed, such as, Who benefits from my labor? The team is proposing a program that gives each department the means to assess whether its business processes effectively meet the needs of internal and external customers.

The team's agenda also includes the following suggestions from Quality Team III:

- Improve management skills in the recognition of individual efforts to improve quality. (We are addressing this through our positive feedback efforts and modifications in our formal awards program and the Koala T. Bear award program.)
- Improve the involvement in and commitment to quality goals and measurement programs by employees in our central office.
- Consider facilitating the review of personal quality goals during performance appraisals. (The majority of our employees believe quality goals should be considered in the performance appraisals of all employees.)

Finally, the quality emphasis has given all of us a sense of pride in the company and in the jobs we do. That sense of pride echoes through the conversations of Tennant Company employees, whether they sit in an office or work on the line. "There's nothing like the feeling of accomplishment from doing a job well. It all boils down to producing a quality product the best way we know how," one employee said.

For another employee, "Quality means working as effectively and efficiently as possible to create growth opportunities for myself and for the company. That makes me feel proud."

One of our assemblers summed it up succinctly. "The quality process has helped us work together and learn to respect each other. And that's how we really improve."

Working on Rework

In 1979, when Tennant Company was just launching the quality emphasis, John Davis, the manager of manufacturing engineering, and I were working on long-range warehousing and production space plans.

Warehousing space is relatively easy to predict by looking at growth trends of new part numbers. The traditional approach to planning for manufacturing space is to measure people capacity, machine capacity, and assembly line capacity, then to compare them to actual historical output.

In measuring people capacity, we counted 20 rework mechanics in manufacturing, one rework person in sheet metal, and a rework station in welding, plus a touch-up paint booth in assembly. It didn't take long to calculate that rework tied up from 6,000 to 10,000 feet of manufacturing floor space.

These rework operations were not unusual to comparable industries, but we realized that if this continued, we would soon need a space the size of a football field to store all the machines waiting to be reworked. We would have *no* space for manufacturing.

How had this happened? It certainly wasn't because the workers wanted it that way. Our people simply performed to expectations set by our managers. But knowing that didn't help much. We still had to figure out how to solve the problem.

At about this time, Phil Crosby made his first visit to Tennant Company. During his tour of the plants, we told him the results of our study and asked for his suggestions.

"It's simple. Build the machines right the first time, and cut the number of rework mechanics in half. I'll stop back in a month to see how you're doing."

You can imagine the looks on our faces. Cut the rework mechanics by 50 percent? They were the highest-paid assemblers. They had the most seniority. They did what we managers told them to do!

We had no idea how to implement Crosby's suggestions. Tennant Company had never laid off any workers. Besides, John and I still had shipment and production goals to meet. We needed a plan that would deal with the problem and make everyone, including the company, happy.

Here was our plan:

1. Reduce the number of rework mechanics on a seniority basis and by asking for volunteers.
2. Reassign people.
3. Eliminate storing machines before rework.
4. Solve quality-related problems on the assembly lines.

In 12 months, we saw the following results:

- Between 6,000 and 8,000 square feet of floor space were freed for production.
- We were able to meet our monthly production and shipping goals.
- Some machines were being built without defects.
- Most people affected agreed with the changes and cooperated as much as they could.

We began to believe that Phil Crosby knew exactly what he meant when he said, "It's simple. Just do things right the first time!" **R.K.**

MANUFACTURING REWORK HOURS

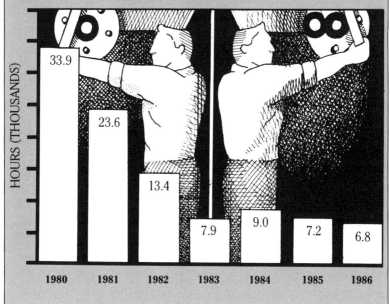

HOURS (THOUSANDS)

1980	1981	1982	1983	1984	1985	1986
33.9	23.6	13.4	7.9	9.0	7.2	6.8

Curing Bonding Failures

Sometimes new technologies are needed to reduce defects. Throughout the 1960s and into the early 1970s, we experienced recurring floor-coating bonding failures. Our customers were not ready to abandon our coatings entirely—they were having similar failures with our competitors. We were the "best of the worst," and the problem was persistent enough that most of our direct sales people were reluctant to sell the product.

Our primary coating for concrete at the time was an epoxy-primer coating product which required a three-step process of thorough cleaning, priming, and coating. It relied on mechanical bonding properties between the concrete and coating, but for some reason many applications simply did not adhere. To compound the problem, it was almost impossible to predict which floors would retain the coating and which floors would reject it.

We're fortunate at Tennant Company to have a team of highly qualified chemists who, in the mid-1970s, knew it was imperative to solve this problem. The chemists knew the major culprit of bonding failures was moisture. It wicks up to the coating bottom and loosens the bond. They recognized that even though concrete looks dry, moisture is often present, especially when the humidity is high, the concrete is new (since water is used to mix and apply it), and when the water table rises.

The first step the chemists took was to more accurately predict when the moisture level was too high. Coatings in the southeastern United States, for example, rarely worked because of the constant high humidity levels, and we knew this was a lost market unless we could do a better job of determining a maximum moisture level.

We took a moisture meter that had been used to read wood wetness and adapted it for use on concrete. Through extensive testing, we determined that any reading beyond a 17 would be unsuitable for our coatings. This was a major breakthrough because it took the guesswork out of deciding which floors would be successful candidates.

But the chemists weren't satisfied. They wanted to overcome the moisture problem by developing a better product. This process took years of trial and error. New testing equipment was purchased. Environmental test facilities were installed, enabling the chemists to simulate different climates and conditions while measuring moisture content and testing scores of potential product improvements.

Finally, in 1979, an improved product was introduced, and it was a technological breakthrough. This is a hybrid concoction that bonds chemically rather than mechanically to concrete. The chemical bond not only enhances the bond strength, but also eliminates the priming step. Floors still need a thorough cleaning, but now the applicator only needs to pour the new mixture into the urethane and apply—the primer is built into the coating.

With this product, floors that exceed the reading limit of 17 can be coated up to a reading of 20 and sometimes higher. The credibility of TENNANT floor coatings was strengthened, and our sales reps are no longer reluctant to sell the product. We rarely see bonding failures now, and most of those we do experience are related to insufficiently cleaned floors. **D.H.**

BONDING FAILURES—FLOOR SEALS

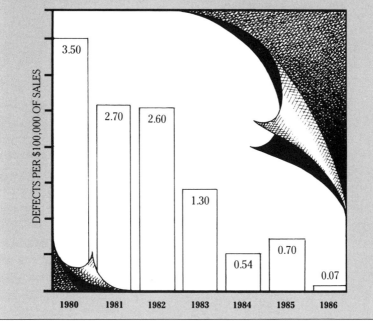

Afterword

If anyone had told us seven years ago that we would write a book, we would have laughed out loud. We consider ourselves students—not teachers.

When we started down the never-ending road to quality, we had no idea how many opportunities would grow from what we were doing. A good example is this book. We decided to write it because of the many requests we've had from other companies for information and sound practical advice.

Over the years, our company has become well known for its quality efforts, thanks in part to Phil Crosby, who often uses us as an example in his writing and when he consults with other companies. But also, the word has simply spread. We began receiving phone calls from people in other companies who wanted to come and find out just how we had accomplished what we had. Before long, we had so many requests we had to set up a regular "visitors' day" each month just for tours and interview sessions.

Then people began asking for some written material that they could take back to their companies. We published a booklet, "Dare to Improve," that we have reprinted by the thousands, and Phil Crosby has used it as a handout in his "Quality College." All over the country, people want to know how to implement a quality process in their companies. And often, the company they look to for help is ours.

We're a little embarrassed by all the attention—and by the implication that we came up with something unique. We didn't. We didn't originate any of the ideas or techniques that have become part of our quality process. They came from many sources; some we adapted from experts like Phil Crosby, W. Edwards Deming, and Joseph Juran; some came from other companies and others from books we read. Many of the best ideas came from Tennant Company employees, the people who do the work.

Because we are indebted to so many for what we have been able to do, we feel it is only right to pass what we have learned on to others. The worst thing we could do is hide it. The more we share, the more we learn. The old principle, "the more you put in, the more you'll get out," certainly applies to quality.

We frequently say that quality is a never-ending process. The better we get, the better we want to get. And we can't get better unless we are continually learning from other companies, as well as from our customers, employees, and suppliers.

We'd like to leave you with one final thought.

All three of us—Ron, Doug, and Roger—share a deep fondness for the great outdoors. One of our common interests is river canoeing, and a favorite river is the Namekagon in northwestern Wisconsin. No matter what time of year we canoe the river, and no matter what the water level is, we always encounter rocks that can cause the canoe to tip or pop a rivet. Each time the water level changes, different rocks become the dangerous ones.

There is an analogy between this river and our quality emphasis. Some of our assumptions about the future are based on experiences from the past, which may not be entirely valid. Just as the water level changes, our problems change, and different issues become the dangerous ones.

We believe the principles we've outlined in this book are going to be with us for a long time—at least as long as we're alive and kicking. During that time, we will work on several areas not mentioned in this book. They are:

- Better understanding of our customers' real needs. (We serve

more than 25,000 customers annually.)
- Doing a better job of meeting those needs.
- Placing a greater emphasis on reliability, which is, simply stated, quality over time.
- A greater emphasis on statistical process control (SPC).
- Placing an even greater emphasis on prevention in the design of products and processes in both the product and administrative functions.

In short, a never-ending effort is required to make Tennant Company "the standard for quality worldwide."

Appendix

TQ **ERROR CAUSE IDENTIFICATION**

ECI # _____
Part # _____

INITIATOR

Date _____   Machine Model _____

Initiator _____   Dept. Name _____   Phone Ext. _____

Problem & Cause _____
_____
_____
_____
_____
_____

Date Problem First Discovered: _____

SUPERVISOR/MANAGER

Manager/Supervisor Comment: _____
_____
_____

Suggested Corrective Action: _____
_____

- Mfg. & Eng. Codes -

1. ☐ (E) Equipment   5. ☐ (M) Material
2. ☐ (IE) IE/Methods   6. ☐ (OP) Op Error
3. ☐ (P) Process   7. ☐ (T) Tooling
4. ☐ (S) Specs   8. ☐ (OT) Other

- Office & Field Codes -

1. ☐ (OP) Order Processing   5. ☐ (S) Systems
2. ☐ (B) Billing   6. ☐ (M) Manufacturing
3. ☐ (E) Engineering   7. ☐ (OI) Other
4. ☐ (P) Purchasing

Evaluator/Department Responsible for Corrective Action: _____

Seriousness:

(a) Ranking (circle one):   Stops vital activities or production   6 5 4 3 2 1   Inconvenient

(b) Dollar Impact and Basis (if known): $_____

(c) Other departments that may be affected: _____

Manager/Supervisor Signature: _____   Date _____

EVALUATOR

1. Original Evaluator _____   Dept. _____

2. Transferred Evaluator _____   Dept. _____

Analysis: _____
_____
_____

Corrective Action Taken: _____
_____
_____
_____

Estimated Implementation Date _____

Indicate the Correct Code Number: _____ Office & Field _____ Mfg. & Eng.

Completed By Evaluator _____   Date _____

Initiators Approval _____   Date _____

E.C.I. Coordinator _____   Date _____

10010683 R

The Quality Improvement Program: Phil Crosby's Fourteen Steps

Step One: **Management Commitment**
Purpose: To make it clear where management stands on quality.
Step Two: **The Quality Improvement Team**
Purpose: To run the quality improvement program.
Step Three: **Quality Measurement**
Purpose: To provide a display of current and potential nonconformance problems in a manner that permits objective evaluation and corrective action.
Step Four: **The Cost of Quality**
Purpose: To define the ingredients of the cost of quality, and explain its use as a management tool.
Step Five: **Quality Awareness**
Purpose: To provide a method of raising the personal concern felt by all personnel in the company toward the conformance of the product or service and the quality reputation of the company.
Step Six: **Corrective Action**
Purpose: To provide a systematic method of resolving forever the problems that are identified through previous action steps.
Step Seven: **Zero Defects Planning**
Purpose: To examine the various activities that must be conducted in preparation for formally launching the Zero Defects program.
Step Eight: **Supervisor Training**
Purpose: To define the type of training that supervisors need in order to actively carry out their part of the quality improvement program.
Step Nine: **ZD Day**
Purpose: To create an event that will let all employees realize, through a personal experience, that there has been a change.
Step Ten: **Goal Setting**
Purpose: To turn pledges and commitments into action by encouraging individuals to establish improvement goals for themselves and their groups.
Step Eleven: **Error-cause Removal**
Purpose: To give the individual employee a method of communicating to management the situations that make it difficult for the employee to meet the pledge to improve.
Step Twelve: **Recognition**
Purpose: To appreciate those who participate.
Step Thirteen: **Quality Councils**
Purpose: To bring together the professional quality people for planned communication on a regular basis.
Step Fourteen: **Do It Over Again**
Purpose: To emphasize that the quality improvement program never ends.

Philip B. Crosby, *Quality is Free* (McGraw-Hill, 1979), pp. 175-259.

Tennant Company
Supplier Qualification
Process

"In our relationships with our suppliers, we expect to improve our communications, not only in the area of quality management but throughout all aspects of our business association ....we are looking for improvement every year .... Our long-range intent is to do business only with qualified suppliers."

"...our attitude toward customer satisfaction and product excellence has forged our statement that Tennant Company is and will continue to be the standard for quality worldwide..."

TENNANT COMPANY
SUPPLIER QUALIFICATION PROCESS

Supplier qualification is the process to identify and qualify those suppliers that Tennant Company is assured will consistently provide materials and processing that will conform to all requirements.

The Purchasing Department is responsible for coordinating the selection of suppliers to be evaluated, for communicating the suppliers' status to them, and for final selection according to the following criteria:

CRITERIA

- On-Site Supplier Assessment
- Supplier Management Quality Conference
- Mutual Understanding of Requirements
- Supplier Corrective Action Request System
- Reliability Performance
- Incoming Lot Performance
- Piece Part Performance
- Delivery Performance

On-Site Supplier Assessment

Purchasing Department and Quality Assurance are jointly responsible for conducting the supplier assessment process. This is an in-depth, on-site investigation of the supplier's management structure and overall business operations.

Purchasing will review the suppliers' physical facilities, manufacturing capabilities, administrative systems, operating and order processing systems, financial analysis, market data, and technical support capabilities. Purchasing will also discuss procedures for returning nonconforming goods assuring that they are well defined, understood, and followed.

Quality Engineering will review the suppliers' quality assurance processes and procedures, quality assurance organization and reporting responsibilities, inspection and test capabilities, calibration and maintenance of gauges and tools, and defect-handling procedures.

Supplier Management Quality Conference

We will discuss Tennant Company's Zero Defects process with supplier's top management and the important role our suppliers play in our corporate quality emphasis. Suppliers are encouraged to share their quality systems with us, and all ideas for mutual improvement will be discussed. It's extremely important that our suppliers understand and share our philosophy of Zero Defects and that they are committed to working with us in achieving this objective.

Mutual Understanding of Requirements

Quality = Conformance to requirements.

All Tennant Company requirements must be clear and understandable to the supplier. All supplier requirements must be clear and understandable to Tennant Company.

Supplier Corrective Action Request System

Tennant Company Supplier Corrective Action Request (SCAR) system must be understood by the supplier and 100% of SCAR's issued must be answered within the specified time period.

Reliability Performance

Reliability is the probability that a product will conform to its specifications throughout its expected life.

Many of our suppliers will be asked to make a commitment to share reliability data with us, to set reliability goals by application, and to work with us in resolving specific reliability problems. These efforts are intended to help us mutually improve the overall reliability of our products.

Incoming Lot Performance

Supplier must meet Tennant Company's goal of 100% accepted incoming lots for either two consecutive six-month reporting periods or one reporting period with more than 100 lots received.

Piece Part Performance

Piece part performance is measured by the number of individual nonconforming parts found after incoming inspection during Tennant Company's manufacturing process.

Supplier must meet Tennant Company's goal for percent Zero Defect piece parts for two consecutive six-month reporting periods. A goal is set for each commodity and will continually increase toward Zero Defects as the commodity as a whole improves.

Supplier must also set an individual company goal in an attempt to continually improve.

Delivery Performance

On-time delivery means no early and no late shipments given adequate lead time. Supplier must meet Tennant Company's goal of 100% on time for the most recent six-month period and 95% on time for the previous six month period.

CATEGORIES

The Purchasing Department evaluates suppliers according to the supplier qualification criteria and classifies suppliers into one of the following categories:

1. Qualified.
2. Conditionally Qualified.
3. Unqualified.

Qualified

A qualified supplier is the highest rating that a supplier can obtain. To achieve this rating, the supplier must meet all of the criteria outlined above.

The Purchasing Department will assign all new parts to qualified suppliers before seeking other sources. Additionally, existing parts will be reassigned to qualified suppliers whenever it is practical to do so.

Conditionally Qualified

A conditionally qualified supplier is a supplier who does not meet one or more of the above listed criteria. A supplier in this classification will be informed of the specific conditions which must be satisfied before moving into qualified status. They will also be informed of the time frame involved for this to take place and the possibility of becoming unqualified if conditions are not met.

It is important to know that new and existing components will not be assigned to suppliers in this category where there are qualified suppliers who can provide such products.

Unqualified

If performance in any of the qualification areas is not at acceptable required levels, **and** if no continuous improvement is occurring, then the supplier will be placed in an unqualified status. These suppliers will receive no consideration for furnishing Tennant Company with new or existing parts. Additionally, steps will be taken over a reasonable period of time to discontinue business relationships.

"There's no real magic to quality performance ...involvement's the key. The only magic is the efforts of you and me...and we need our supplier's active involvement in order for Tennant Company to succeed."

Douglas R. Hoelscher
Vice President Engineering,
Manufacturing, and Purchasing

Date: _____   Person Nominated: _____

To: Quality Recognition Committee   Group Nominated: _____

From: _____ (Nominator)   File Number: _____

Title: _____

Phone Extension: _____

Quality Recognition Nomination Form
(Individual and Group)

Objective: To recognize employees who demonstrate
continued quality performance.

Instructions For Nominator: Please read the Criteria for Recognition listed below before making your nomination. These are the criteria which will be used to evaluate nominations for quality recognition awards.

- **Write the name of the person or group you're nominating on the appropriate line at the top of this form**. Use a separate form for each person or group nominated. You may be contacted for additional information related to this nomination.

- Write the names of other persons you suggest be contacted for information about this person or group's performance (try to write at least two names).

Names of other persons to contact: _____

_____

Criteria For Individual Recognition

- Continuous superior performance in doing work right the first time over a minimum of one year.

- Cooperative, positive approach to problem-solving.

- Taking the initiative in corrective action to solve problems (identifying errors, determining cause of errors, correcting errors, or preventing errors).

- Setting quality goals and demonstrating high-level effort to attain goals.

- Communications and other actions support the Quality Program.

Criteria For Group Recognition

- Continuous superior performance in doing work right the first time.

- Taking the initiative in corrective action to solve problems (identifying errors, determining cause of errors, correcting errors, or preventing errors).

- Setting quality goals and demonstrating high-level effort to attain goals.

KOALA T. BEAR AWARD

NOMINATION FORM

OBJECTIVE: To provide on-going recognition, separate from the Formal Recognition program, for consistent performance over a period of time of less than one year, or for a specific project/task.

INSTRUCTIONS: Please read the **CRITERIA FOR RECOGNITION** listed below before making your nomination.

These are the criteria which will be used to evaluate nominations for the Koala T. Bear Award.

CRITERIA FOR RECOGNITION

The employee must:

1. Consistently meet job standards, **and**
2. Have a positive work attitude, **and**
3. Put forth **extra effort** in **at least one** of the following areas:

    A. Output, **or**
    B. Quality, **or**
    C. Efficiency

NOMINEE: _____
            (Name)   (Department)   (Ext.)

NOMINATOR: _____
            (Name)   (Department)   (Ext.)

In addition to the above criteria, who benefits from the nominee's good work? (These people will be asked to provide input in the evaluation of the nominee.)

_____
    (Name)   (Department)   (Ext.)

_____
    (Name)   (Department)   (Ext.)

THANK YOU FOR YOUR NOMINATION!

Please send this form to the Special Projects Committee, attention: Marta Vosberg.

Date Received: _____ Date Evaluated: _____
Meets Criteria _____ Does Not Meet Criteria _____

TENNANT®

SUGGESTION FORM

Date Rec. _____ No. _____

Cost Savings...Stop Waste At Tennant...Mr. C.S. SWAT

NAME _____

DEPT. _____

SUBJECT _____

(Print Neatly-Press Hard With Pen)

DATE _____

(Please follow the instructions on the back of the green form)

CURRENT METHOD OR CONDITION IS: (INCLUDE PART # _____) _____

_____

_____

_____

I SUGGEST THAT: _____

_____

_____

_____

(Attach any sketches, marked up prints, or other information which may help communicate your idea)

MY SUGGESTION WILL AFFORD THESE IMPROVEMENTS OR SAVINGS: _____

_____

_____

_____

SIGNATURE _____

(Forward to your supervisor for eligibility)

DO NOT WRITE BELOW THIS LINE

SUPERVISOR: (All questions must be completed before submitting to Suggestion Chairman for evaluation)
(Before answering, read Eligibility Section on back of green form)

Should this be an ECI? _____
Is the suggestion eligible? _____ Is the suggester eligible? _____
Is the idea workable? _____
Is all available pertinent information clearly shown or attached? _____
Additional comments: _____
_____
_____

Date _____ Signature _____

(DO NOT SEPARATE ATTACHED SHEETS)

EVALUATION SUMMARY:

Date Acted Upon _____

Suggestion: Accepted _____
Check

Rejected _____
Check

Follow-Up _____
Date

Award: Points _____
And/Or

Amount $_____

Signature _____

Training Summary

Year **Description**
1980 Introduction to 14-step Zero-Defect Process
Quality Awareness
Manager/supervisor role for ZD Day
1981 Quality Measurements
Quality Goals
Cost of Quality
1982 Recognition
Hydraulics
Communication—Listening
Problem-solving Techniques
1983 Communication—Working Together
Hydraulics
Problem-solving Techniques
Communication–Listening
1984 Group Process Skills
Hydraulics
Quality Measurements, Goal Setting, and Cost of Quality
Communication–Listening
Torque Control Training on Fasteners
Problem-solving Techniques
Just-In-Time
Communication—Working Together
1985 Intermediate Blueprint
Group Process Skills
Just-In-Time
Geometric Tolerancing
Torque Control
Basic Blueprint Reading
Communication–Working Together
Group Process Follow-up
1986 Torque Control
Value Analysis
Group Process Skills
Statistical Process Control
Negotiation Skills
Problem Solving
Intermediate Blueprint
Geometric Tolerancing
Group Process Follow-up
Creative Thinking
Communication–Working Together
Just-In-Time

Index

NOTES

NOTES

NOW AVAILABLE–*Quest for Quality* video tape

This interview-filled video shows the real inner workings of an effective quality process. With a foreword by Tom Peters, this 45-minute tape can serve as both a model for starting a quality-improvement process and an example for those wanting to rejuvenate a company's current commitment. The *Quest for Quality* video becomes a how-to model for training and increasing awareness.

Here's what some viewers have said:

Tennant Company has provided a great service to America by producing this video tape. It gives other organizations the opportunity to relate to an actual example instead of theoretical concepts presented by consultants. This tape shows a broad representation of real-world people telling their story.
Ronald Modreski, director of quality,
Vickers Inc., AMD Division

The Tennant Company story has been encouraging by helping us realize quality really isn't an isolated effort but a long journey. We've also found the tape serves as an effective motivational tool. It allows us to take a deep breath and see what can happen if we just stick to it.
Marlene Reisner, quality improvement coordinator,
Westinghouse Elevator Company

– –

YES, I want to see *Quest for Quality!*
(Only available in VHS format)

☐ I would like to purchase the tape at $395.
Includes 45-minute video, one book, shipping and handling.

☐ I would like to rent the tape for 5 business days at $125.
Includes 45-minute video, purchase price of one book, shipping and handling.

☐ Please include _____ extra books at $10.95 each

All orders MUST BE accompanied by payment. Rental costs may be applied to the purchase price.

Allow 3 weeks for delivery.

Name _____

Title _____

Company _____

Address _____

City _____ State _____ Zip _____

Telephone (_____) _____

Send this order with payment to:
Tennant Company
Quest for Quality
P.O. Box 1271
Minneapolis, MN 55440
(612) 540-1562

Order extra copies of *Quest for Quality* by completing the order form below and returning it with your payment to:

Tennant Company
Quest for Quality
P.O. Box 1271
Minneapolis, MN 55440
(612) 540-1562

Price List:

1–10 . . . .$10.95 each
11 or more . . . .$ 9.95 each

Price includes handling and sales tax for *each* book.

Qty.		Price
	1 to 10 books @ $10.95 each	
	11 or more @ $9.95 each	
	Total	

Name _____

Title _____

Company _____

Address _____

City _____ State _____ Zip _____

Phone _____

Payment must accompany ALL orders
Make checks payable to TENNANT COMPANY BOOK OFFER